WHITE STAR
PUBLISHERS

Provence

PLACES AND HISTORY

Texts
Silvana Rizzi

Editorial coordination
Giulia Gaida

Graphic design
Anna Galliani

Translation
C.T.M., Milan
Richard Pierce

ISBN 88-8095-695-7
1 2 3 4 5 6   05 04 03 02 01

Printed in Italy by Grafedit

CONTENTS

*1 Known since
ancient times for its
therapeutic
properties, lavender is
now an important
source of income for
the region. Every year
almost one hundred
tons of distilled essence
of lavender are used
for perfumes and
cosmetics.*

*2-7 View of Avignon
and the Pont Bénézet
painted by Isidore
Dagnan in 1833. The
bridge, a symbol of the
city, was built in the
12th century and was
destroyed and rebuilt
several times over the
centuries.*

*3-6 The Papal Palace,
with its massive walls,
square towers and
medieval crenellation.
The first part to be
built was the austere
Palais-Vieux, or Old
Palace, at the behest of
Pope Benedict XII. The
Palais-Neuf was built
later by Pope Clement
VI.*

INTRODUCTION

8 On the Vaucluse plateau around Sault, the village of honey, almonds and nougat, the fields of lavender in bloom seem to be paying a tribute to the wild barrenness of Mt. Ventoux and the mountains of Lure, where aromatic herbs reign supreme.

8-9 The Sault area is a spectacular blend of lavender, kitchen gardens and Saltus oak woods that once covered the entire territory. In fact, this delightful town with mild climate near the Nesque river was named after the oak tree.

9 top left In all of Provence the fields of sunflowers alternate with the olive groves and vineyards. Van Gogh was enchanted by them and painted their glorious yellow with the aim of celebrating a world that fascinated him with its blaze of colors.

A land of scents, sea, mountains and wind. A land exalted by painters and poets. Claude Monet came here to find the light that shines on his water lilies, Pablo Picasso chose Vallauris to be the site of a pottery, Georges Braque adored the countryside of Estaque around Marseilles which was where his ideas that developed into Cubism were inspired, and Mont Sainte-Victoire was made famous around the world by twelve paintings by Paul Cézanne, each of which de-picted it in a different light.

With its clear, pure blue sky regularly swept by the mistral, Provence never fails to delight the traveler in search of emotions. From the enchanted clearness of the water in the fountain of Saint-Paul to the pale green of the sea at dawn when sea and coast merge like the colors of Cézanne and Bonnard. In contrast to the infinite shades of the water, there is the dazzling white limestone of the Calanques, the ochre earth at Roussillon, the dark green of the cluster pines, the golden yellow of the sunflowers and the paler yellow of the mimosa. Everywhere in Provence, the subtle smells of thyme, rosemary and mastic trees permeate the air, but it is the intense perfume of lavender that strikes one at the start of summer and blue carpets welcome the visitor to the magnificent abbey of Sénanque and the village of Sault that nestles between Monieux and Lagarde d'Apt. The gentle silver-grey landscapes of olive trees alternate with steep rocky walls, like the Grand Canyon of Verdon, the deepest in Europe and often compared to its namesake in Colorado. Such physical drama is contrasted by the gentle tranquillity of medieval hilltop villages with their twisting, narrow streets lined with cobbles, their houses roofed with round tiles colored with a pale pink that is seen nowhere else, and each with a small central square bordered by centuries-old plane trees where the locals play *pétanque*.

Examples are Gordes, Saint-Paul

*9 top right
Provence is the
domain of lavender.
In late spring and
summer, the Valensole
plain, between the
Durance river and
the foothills of the
Alps at Digne, is
laden with the scent
of the lovely violet-
mauve lavender
flowers that cover the
earth like a soft,
endless cushion.*

irises were the love of Van Gogh.

For those who prefer bustle and liveliness to the silence of the inland villages, the short trip to the coast is all that is needed to enter the cosmopolitan atmosphere of the crowded port towns. The most famous of all, Saint-Tropez, "a charming and simple daughter of the sea" as defined by Guy de Maupassant in 1888 when he first visited, continues to bewitch the traveler with its famous Tahiti beach and ancient streets.

The worldliness of Saint-Tropez is countered by the simplicity of small ports like Bandol filled with brightly colored fishing boats.

The less well-known coastline between Cassis and Marseilles still has spectacular surprises in store for the first-time traveler: deep, narrow inlets are separated by limestone outcrops that rise perpendicularly from the sea

10 bottom right
The bay of Port-Cros, the islet east of Porquerolles, gives the impression of being in the ocean rather than in the Mediterranean Sea. This is the ideal starting point for excursions into the interior to discover the rich vegetation.

11 The highly indented coastline of the Hyères Islands consists of cliffs, gullies and tiny coves. The luxuriant slopes descend to the unpolluted sea. Of the three islands, Ile du Levant is the most unspoiled.

10 top left
Hundreds of stilt-plovers feed in the shallow waters of the Estang de Vaccarès in the Camargue.

10 bottom left
In the Camargue marshes herons, flamingos, diving ducks, cormorants and white herons live in harmony with the famous local horses.

10 top right
At Cassis the pure blue sea seems to be embraced by the enchanting, tranquil bay.

de Vence, Tourrettes, Biot, Apt, Moustiers and Bormes-les-Mimosas to name but a few. These villages are announced from afar by the tower of a castle or a church with an elegant wrought iron cage in the shape of a prism containing, as if suspended in space, a bell. Its knells echo throughout the local villages whenever the wind blows. At one time they served as a warning to the villagers that the mistral was on its way and that they should shut themselves up in their houses with windows and doors barred. More intimate and retiring is the Lubéron where every Parisian dreams of having a *mas*: its ochre walls and gentle hills covered with olive trees, lavender and

12 top
The charming village of Roussillon is perched on the crest of a hill facing the ochre quarries. Seventeen shades of this earthy iron oxide color the surrounding landscape. In the past the natural ochre pigment extracted here was used for painting houses.

12-13 Les Baux-de-Provence attracts more visitors every year than the Louvre. Tourists are enchanted by the centuries-old streets with old buildings and by the medieval village that was built on the spur of white rock flanked by craggy gorges.

and are topped by tufts of green. Lovers of unspoiled nature will enjoy the three Hyères islands where cars are forbidden and travel among the thick pinewoods is all on foot or by bicycle: the first, Porquerolles, was the setting for one of Georges Simenon's most famous detective stories, *Mon ami Maigret*, and is a safe shelter for sailors; then there is the national park on Port-Cros and the island of Levant.

The wild, lonely Camargue is a flat wetland of canals and marshes that fan out into the estuary of the Rhône. The Camargue is home to flocks of pink flamingos that suddenly rise up into the air from the marshes, wild horses and dark-colored bulls with lyre-shaped horns that are overseen by the *gardians*, the cowboys of France. At the end of May, gypsies arrive at Saintes-Marie-de-la-Mer from all over Europe to celebrate the festival of Saint Sarah, the black patron saint of the *gitans*.

The visitor in search of antiquities will find extraordinary sites. The roots of great cities like Marseilles, boastful and irreverent, home of Marcel Pagnol and Fernandel, grew out of the Greek civilization but most of all it was the genius of imperial Rome that has left its mark throughout Provence. Orange has one of the best known amphitheaters; Arles (the "merveilleuse petite ville" according to Alphonse Daudet in 1869) boasts a splendid arena, while Saint-Rémy is famous for its Antiques, the french name for the archeological site of the ancient roman town Glanum. The artistic atmosphere found just about everywhere in Provence is celebrated with superb galleries and museums, large and small, in cities and villages, for example, Arles Antique, the Maeght collection, the Vasarély museum in Gordes, the Petit Palais in Avignon and the Léger museum in Biot.

What marks the borders of Provence? As part of the French region Provence-Alpes-Côte d'Azur, the territory strictly only covers the departments of Bouches-du-Rhône, the Var and the Alpes-de-Haute-Provence but its heart beats in Vaucluse and Drôme all the way down to Grasse and Saint-Paul-de-Vence which were owned by the Counts of Provence up till the end of the 15th century.

16-17 At Salin-de-Giraud and west of the Petit Rhône, in the Camargue, lie the geometric salt works. Sea water is pumped onto the evaporation tables and leveled by small dams. At sunset the surface of these basins is covered with fascinating reddish hues.

18-19 The coves at Sormiou and Morgiou, in the vicinity of Marseilles, are popular with excursionists. These white rocks with patches of typical Mediterranean brush and maritime pines plunge headlong into the sea, going as deep as 328 feet below the surface.

The ochre earth at Roussillon

View of Les Baux

Ile du Levant, Hyères

Vaucluse

▲
Mount
Ventoux

Rodano

•Orange

•Carpentras

•Avignon

Lubéron

•Saint Rémy-
de Provence

•Arles Les Alpilles

Durance

Aix
en-Provence

Aigues-Mortes

Etang de
Vaccarès

Etang
de Berre

Montagne
Sainte-Victoire

•Camargue

Bouches-du-
Rhône

•Marseilles

Vineyards in the Barroux area

Barcelonnette

Ubaye

Alpes-de-
Haute-Provence

zron

Digne-les-Bains

Var

Verdon

Alpes Maritimes

Vence

Grasse

Massif
de l'Esterel

Argens

Côte d'Azur

Var

Massif
des Maures

Saint Tropez

on

Hyères

Hyères Islands

The Arch of Augustus, St-Rémy-de-Provence

Pelicans at Camargue

AN ENDURING LAND (THROUGH MILLENIUMS)

20 top The Avignon Epigraphic Museum, one of the richest and most interesting of its kind in France, has this tablet with inscriptions in Greek and Celtic that bear witness to the contact between these two cultures.

The history of Provence is fascinating. Like a huge stage that opens onto the Mediterranean, the region bears the imprint of every epoch: Roman remains, medieval villages and elegant renaissance palaces. A thin thread connects the various stages of Provence's past, it is the spirit of independence that the region has always shown during the fundamental moments of its history.

The earliest remains worthy of note were immortalized in the fascinating rock-paintings around 2000 BC in the Vallée des Merveilles in the Alpes-Maritimes. The most important event, however, took place in 600 BC when a group of Greek colonizers, the Phocaeans, left the coasts of Asia Minor in search of a Mediterranean port that would allow them to control the tin market. Protected from the winds and supplied with excellent water sources, Massalia (modern day Marseilles) seemed the ideal spot. The new arrivals established solid relations with the local Celtic-Ligurian population to the point of sealing the friendship with the marriage of Protis, leader of the Phocaeans, to Gyptis, a member of a Celtic tribe. Massalia remained independent for five centuries from that time becoming a prosperous and well-known city. The Phocaeans introduced olives, figs, cherries and grapes as well as the concept of money. Able dealers, they instituted trading centers – the famous *comptoirs* – at Hyères, Saint-Tropez, Antibes, Nice and Monaco. From Massalia, Greek culture conquered the Liguri tribe that inhabited the nearby villages. Coins, pottery and Massalian culture spread inland and up the Rhône valley as is evidenced by the statues displayed in the Granet museum in Aix and the Archaeological Museum in Marseilles. The modern inhabitants of Arles still declare that the beauty and grace of their women is derived from their ancient Greek blood.

20 bottom In the Vallée des Merveilles, west of Tende, in the Maritime Alps region, the splendid rock paintings scattered here and there illustrate the primitive life of the people who lived here in 2000 B.C. These paintings, which are not without artistic value, evoke a world that is only apparently remote in time.

P. Puvis de Chavannes. 1869

20-21 The left wing of Palais Longchamp in Marseilles is the home of the Fine Arts Museum, the majestic staircase of which is decorated with two canvases by Pierre Puvis de Chavannes: Marseilles, *a Greek Colony (above) and Gate to the East. An exceptional colorist, Puvis de Chavannes here recreates a combination of the golden age of Greek civilization and a vision of an enchanting Orient that is perhaps tinged with dream fantasy.*

21 bottom
A two-headed sculpture of the god Hermes, who was worshipped by travelers and merchants whose trade often obliged them to face the unknown. This Celtic work of obvious Greek inspiration betrays an art that has not yet found the equanimity that would distinguish it in a later age. The double head symbolizes the glance of the god that looks in every direction to observe a world that is yet to be explored.

The wealth of Massalia quickly drew the interest of the Romans who began to create trading relations with the city during the fourth century BC. They were so well developed by the end of the second century BC that the Massalians asked help from the Romans to fight a coalition of Celtic and Liguri tribes that were attempting to take the city. Having arrived as peace-makers, in 122 BC the Romans founded a new city, Aquae Sixtiae, named after the consul Sextius Calvinus, which is today known as Aix-en-Provence. Then the Provincia Narbonese was created which took its name from Narbonne, the important center in the region. Seventy years later, in 49 BC, Julius Caesar inflicted the coup

de grace on Massalia, already weakened by trading competition with its neighbors. The city, guilty of having supported Marius in the struggle against Caesar for political supremacy in Rome, fell definitively into ruin. This was instead the fortune of nearby Arles, which from this moment on became the preferred city of the Romans. They built the walls, the splendid arena (still used for bull-fighting), the baths, the forum and the Via Aurelia that connected Spain to Rome. In addition, and most important of all, they built the bridge made of boats across the Rhône which was to remain a means of communication of major importance for almost a thousand years. Arles is the city that mostly fo-

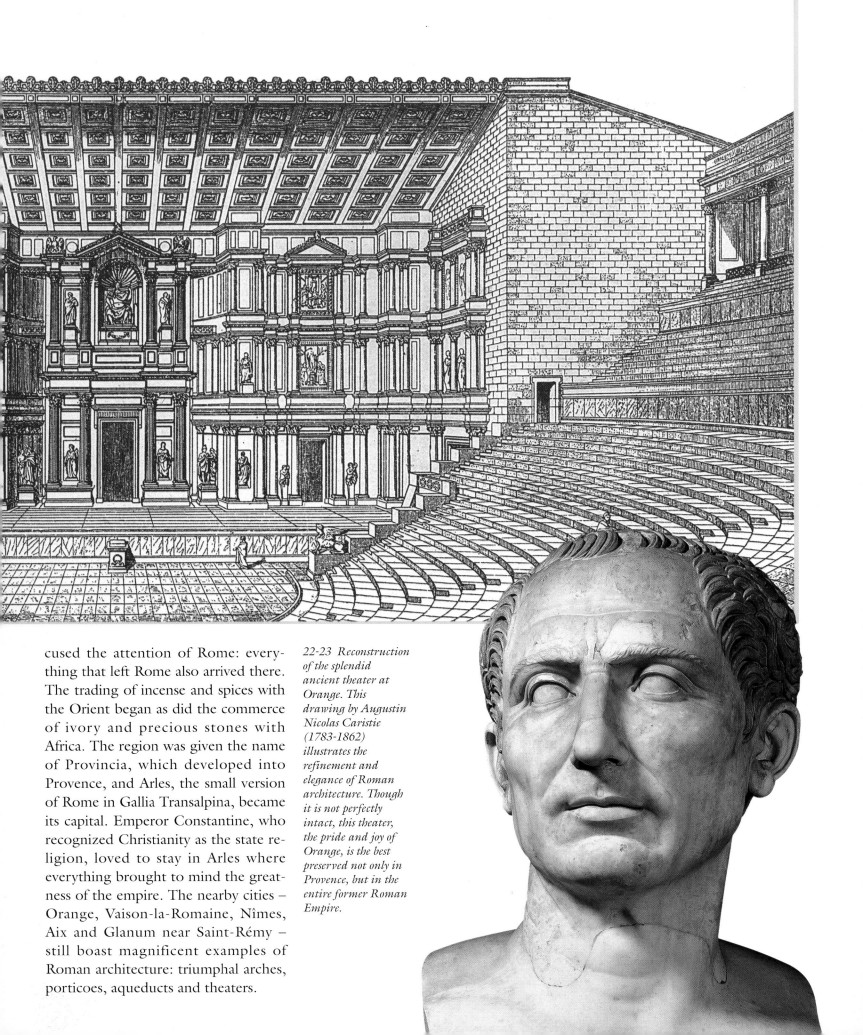

cused the attention of Rome: everything that left Rome also arrived there. The trading of incense and spices with the Orient began as did the commerce of ivory and precious stones with Africa. The region was given the name of Provincia, which developed into Provence, and Arles, the small version of Rome in Gallia Transalpina, became its capital. Emperor Constantine, who recognized Christianity as the state religion, loved to stay in Arles where everything brought to mind the greatness of the empire. The nearby cities – Orange, Vaison-la-Romaine, Nîmes, Aix and Glanum near Saint-Rémy – still boast magnificent examples of Roman architecture: triumphal arches, porticoes, aqueducts and theaters.

22-23 Reconstruction of the splendid ancient theater at Orange. This drawing by Augustin Nicolas Caristie (1783-1862) illustrates the refinement and elegance of Roman architecture. Though it is not perfectly intact, this theater, the pride and joy of Orange, is the best preserved not only in Provence, but in the entire former Roman Empire.

L'AMPHITEATRE D'ARLES COMME IL EST A PRESEN

Etait encore en 1824 époque ou on en   Commença Le Déblaiement qui f
en 1929   L'honneur à M.r Languis, Baron de   Chartrouse à qui la ville d'arles recomman
est mort Dans le mois de novembre 1843 —

With the fall of the empire and the end of the *Pax Romana* during the fifth century, the future of Provincia also became uncertain. The end of Roman protection opened the floodgates to the Visigoths who destroyed Arles in 471. Provence was by that time known as the land of sun and abundance and as a true garden of Eden so its fortunes made it a desirable target for the greed of many other peoples. By the time the Saracens arrived, incursions were the order of the day. Despite having been sacked, the rich city of Arles continued to enjoy a certain comfort until the eighth century when the Moors destroyed the city's lifeline, its bridge over the Rhône. Only in the year 974, two hundred years after the victory

of Charles Martel at Poitiers, the duke of Arles, Guillaume, chased the Saracens out of Freinet, which had been their final resting place. As liberator, Guillaume was granted the noble title of "Marquis de Provence" and this marked the beginning of the feudal era. Country folk built their houses around the castles and monasteries so creating the first fortified villages perched on hilltops safe from invaders. Religious life during this era was exemplified by the construction of magnificent abbeys like the Benedictine Montmajour near Arles and the Cistercian Sénanque and Sylvacane. The region began to enjoy strong economic development but the

25 left
The statue of
Raymond V of
Tolouse—the last
Catalan count, who
was crowned in Aix-
en-Provence—is in
Rochefort du Gard.

25 right This statue
of a first century
barbarian soldier was
found in Avignon
and is now kept in the
Museum of Roman
Civilization, Rome.

24-25 In order to
defend themselves from
the Saracens, in the
Middle Ages the
citizens of Arles used
the massive walls of the
Roman amphitheater
as ramparts and built
a citadel inside them.

24 bottom In the ninth
and tenth century the
Saracens invaded and
sacked Marseilles,
Arles, as well as many
villages and
monasteries. They
conquered Freinet,
using it as a base to
make raids throughout
France.

lineage of the counts of Provence was weakened by a continuous line of females so that in 1125, the territory was divided into two parts: one went to the Catalan count, Raymond Berengar, while the section north of the river Durance became the property of the count of Toulouse who purchased it as the marquisate of Provence. Regardless of the division of the territory, the feuds between lords for dominion of the province did not cease until 1229 when the *Paix de Paris* gave the dukedom of Narbonne and the viscounty of Carcassonne to the crown of France. All lands to the west of the Rhône remained the property of Raymond Berengar V who established himself at Aix-en-Provence.

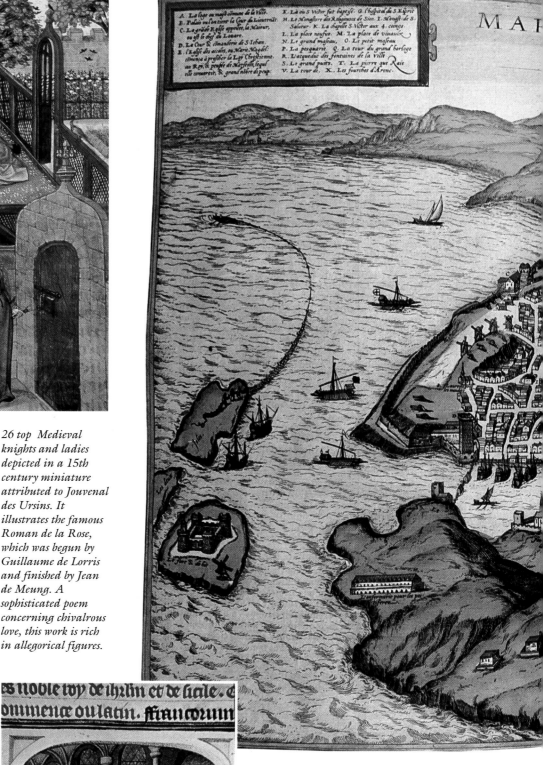

Economic development during the 12th and 13th centuries was strong: villages and the population grew and many cities founded by the Romans, such as Vaison, grew considerably. Others along the main paths of communication, like Tarascon and Draguignan, also increased in size. Trade increased at Arles and Avignon and craftsmen grew richer. The port of Marseilles during the Crusades assumed a role of notable importance thanks to Richard Lionheart who departed from the city in 1190 on the Third Crusade. Linen arrived in Marseilles from Flanders and nearby Languedoc for exchange with spices, silk and precious stones arriving from the mysterious East. Despite the struggles with the counts of Provence, the hilltop town of Les Baux that dominated the Val d'enfer was the center of a brilliant and refined court. Here, around 1150, Etienne des Baux, the brilliant wife of Raymond I des Baux, created the *Cours d'Amours*, the first feminist meetings in history. During the meetings, illustrious women of high birth set down the rules of courtly love and discussed the art of loving.

26 top Medieval knights and ladies depicted in a 15th century miniature attributed to Jouvenal des Ursins. It illustrates the famous Roman de la Rose, which was begun by Guillaume de Lorris and finished by Jean de Meung. A sophisticated poem concerning chivalrous love, this work is rich in allegorical figures.

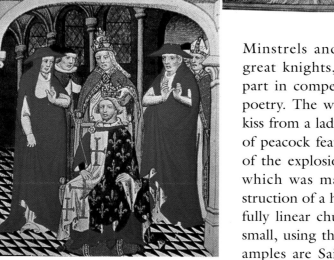

Minstrels and troubadours, often great knights, were invited to take part in competitions of singing and poetry. The winners were awarded a kiss from a lady at court and a crown of peacock feathers. This was the era of the explosion of Romanesque art which was manifested in the construction of a huge number of beautifully linear churches, both large and small, using the local pink stone. Examples are Saint-Trophime in Arles

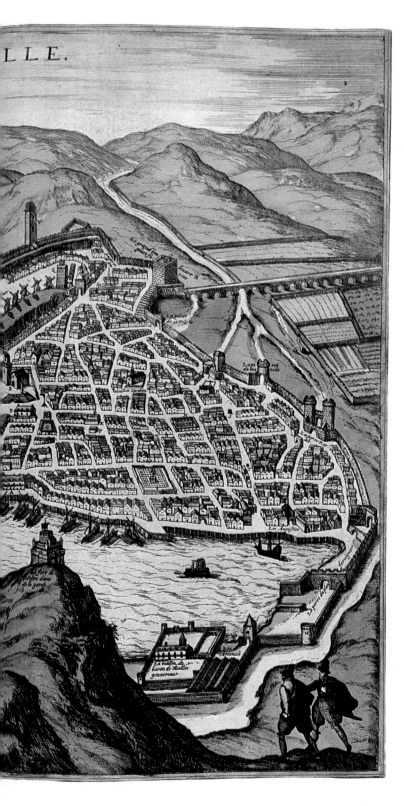

LLE.

called the "four queens" – brought new alliances that took Provence into the sphere of French influence. Margherita, with whom the troubadour Rambaud d'Orange fell head over heels in love and for which he was exiled to Porquerolles, married the king of France, Louis IX, St. Louis. The youngest, Béatrix, was awarded Provence and in 1246 married Charles of Anjou, the brother of Louis IX. The new lord of Provence, busy in the Crusades, allowed the large angry cities such as Arles, Marseilles and Avignon to claim independence but the illusion was short-lived. On his return, Charles took the situation in hand and began systematic reconquest of his power. To make his dominion more secure economically, he implemented a tax on salt, which brought him so much it represented half of all his income. Provence was more fortunate under his successors Charles II and Robert who turned out to be good administrators and well-disposed towards the region. They gave the cities the freedom to form their own city councils and the right

26-27 This view of Marseilles in the 16th century in an engraving by Franz Hogenberg, is from Le Théâtre du Monde *by Georg Braun (1599). The leading port town in France at the time, the city was a veritable entranceway for the many pestilences that periodically decimated the population. In the lower left-hand corner is the building where those who seemed to have the plague were confined.*

27 bottom Louis IX, the saint who was king of France in 1226-70, in a miniature. At left he is in front of the baptismal font, while at right he is portrayed together with his wife Margaret of Provence. A monarch who was popular because of his sense of justice and his virtue, Louis died of the plague in Tunis in 1270 after having taken part in the first two Crusades.

26 bottom A 13th century French school miniature shows Pope Clement IV crowning Charles I of Anjou.

with its magnificent portal decorated with scenes from the life of Jesus, and the picturesque chapel of Sainte Blaise in Les Baux, built for the fraternity of weavers and carders that used to meet there. The Benedictine abbeys of Montmajour and Saint-Victor grew ever richer and more important thanks to munificent donations. Raymond Berengar V died without leaving a male heir but the marriages of his four daughters –

to independent administration.

Meanwhile Avignon, the ancient Avenius, "the city of the river and the wind" founded in the second century BC on detritus accumulated during a flood of the river Rhône, revealed itself after decades of ruin to be one of the most open, most cultured and richest attractions in the area, ready to take advantage of an unexpected event. In the 14th century, the Holy See was oppressed by various political factions in Rome and, unable to cope with internal intrigues, Pope Clement V, originally from France and protected by Philippe le Beau, decided to take shelter in France in a Dominican monastery in Avignon. It was the start of the city's fortune, which welcomed seven French popes between 1309 and 1377. Then, as it had no seat worthy of Christ's representative on earth, Benedict XII built the austere Palais Vieux complete with towers and crenellations with the aid of architect Pierre Poisson de Mirepoix. Clement VI completed the construction of the palace and entrusted the building of the Palais Nouveau to Jean de Louvres who produced a

28 Avignon and the Papal Palace in a 14th century miniature. It was Pope Clement V who had the Papal See moved to Avignon and suppressed the Knights Templars order. During the 14th century the papal court at Avignon became a flourishing cultural center that influenced the entire region.

29 top This miniature, part of a 14th century manuscript now kept in Madrid, represents Pope John XXII surrounded by the clergy.

29 bottom Miniature by Pierre Roger from Giovanni Villani's New Chronicle *depicting the coronation of Pope Clement VI.*

magnificent example of Gothic architecture. Moreover, tired of being a perpetual guest in the city, the Pope bought the entire city of Avignon from Queen Joanna, countess of Provence, in 1348.

As can be imagined, in spite of the plague that killed thousands of victims that same year, the stay of the popes made the 14th century the golden age for Avignon. The city was transformed and increased in size. The bishop had a new impressive residence built, the nobles constructed towers and Gothic palaces and religious buildings were renovated. As an artistic and intellectual capital and with the most admired faculty of law in Europe, Avignon had a cultural life of stature dominated by Francesco Petrarch who lived there from 1311. Tradesmen prospered. Pope John XXII (1316-34) encouraged the cultivation of vines – one of the riches of the region – and created the reputation of the vineyards of Châteauneuf-du-Pape.

On the return of the popes to Rome, a long period of internal struggles and raids followed that culminated in the sacking of Marseilles in 1423. A further ten years of disorder continued until peace was restored under King René of Anjou who turned his back on the kingdom of Naples and chose Aix-en-Provence as his seat. Many stories have been told about this king who has gone down in history as "good king René." On the one hand, he loved the arts and culture, wrote poetry and protected artists but, on the other, he was greedy, always in need of money and did not hesitate to tax his subjects hard.

On his death in 1480, Provence was destined to lose its autonomy. The next king, Charles III of Maine, ruled only for a few months before leaving the land to his cousin Louis XI, king of France. Aware of the strong attachment of the Provençal people to their independence, the French instituted a parliament in Provence in 1501 based on the model of the parliament in Paris but with the obligation that the Provençal version should deal with their various problems in the same manner as was done in Paris. The iron

30 top Louis XI portrayed in a miniature by Jean de Valognes in the Chronique de Louis XI, *now kept in the Bibliothèque Nationale, Paris. The king of France in 1461-83, Louis was absolutist, avid and involved in intrigues,* *and was opposed by many feudal lords whose privileges he wanted to curb. On August 20, 1468 Louis decreed the death sentence of the enemy of the Crown, Charles of Melun, the lord of Normanville.* *30 bottom Avignon in an old map by Ignazio Danti. Surrounded by a wall and by the Rhône river, the city is here still linked with Villenueve-lès-Avignon by the Saint-Bénézet bridge.*

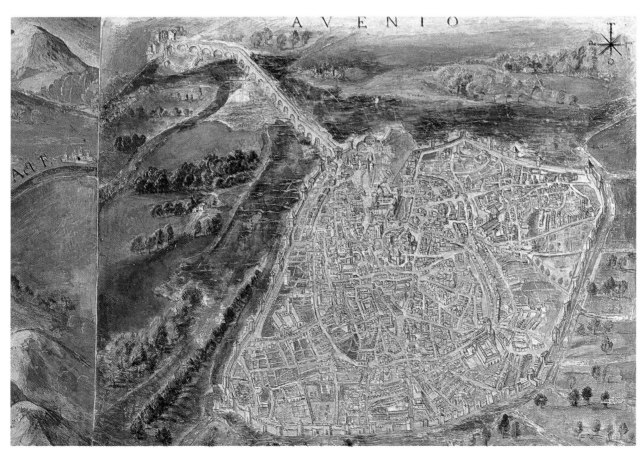

30-31 This splendid miniature, The Skirmish, *from René of Anjou's* Book of Tournaments *(1465), illustrates this major medieval event that involved knights, poets, cantors and lovely ladies.*

31 bottom René of Anjou and his second wife are portrayed in this diptych by Forment (1475). The "Good King" was a poet, musician and man of letters who was loved for his character but hated for the heavy taxes he imposed. He ruled Naples in 1438-42 and later set up his court in Tarascon.

fist of Paris shortly made itself apparent, however. Many Jewish communities lived in southern France at that time with their own schools and synagogues; they also created work for many butchers in requiring their meat to be cut in accordance with the dictates of their religion. At the start of the 16th century, a directive was issued by Paris that gave no choice to the Jews of Provence but to either convert or to emigrate. Some requested asylum in the Comté-Venaisson, the lands belonging to the Papacy, which also welcomed those Jews exiled from Languedoc and the Dauphinate. Only the Jews living in Avignon remained untouched although they were obliged to live in certain closed streets and to wear a yellow cap so that they might be recognized.

At the end of the 15th and start of the 16th centuries, Provence was involved in wars undertaken by the monarchs of France against Italy. Marseilles and Toulon were two strategically important bases from which expeditions set out against the Bel Paese but the French military operation soon backfired on Provence: in 1524, Charles V, the "Holy Roman Emperor," marched on Toulon and Aix and took both cities. It fell to the French king, Francis I, to put the emperor back in his place, which he did in 1536, and to strengthen the borders of the territory that marked the entrance to a powerful kingdom.

The religious wars between Catholics and Protestants that devastated France in the 16th century did not spare Provence. One of the few cities not to be involved was Orange as it had been inherited by the Dutch family, the counts of Nassau, who defended the city's Protestantism.

The same parliament in Aix seemed to follow the directives of the Parisian parliament and prepared itself to condemn the doctrine of the Huguenots. When the abbey of Sénanque was sacked by Protestants in 1544, the reaction of the Catholics was of unparalleled violence: the vil-

lages in which Huguenots were known to live were burned to the ground and over 3000 people were killed. Moving against the current of the times, as always, Marseilles allied itself with the Protestants and only yielded when Casaulx, the leader of the city, was assassinated in 1596. When King Henri IV was informed of the fact, he sighed with relief and exclaimed, "Now I am king of France". Two years later, the Edict of Nantes gave the Huguenots freedom of worship and the massacres came to an end.

32 top Pope Clement VII speaking with Francis I in a painting by Giorgio Vasari and his pupils. The French king understood the strategic importance of Provence and reinforced its borders.

32 bottom This work, also by Vasari and pupils, portrays Clement VII and Charles V. The emperor tried to conquer Provence in 1524 but was defeated in 1536.

32-33 A splendid painting of the city of Marseilles by an anonymous 15th-16th century artist.

33 top left The territory of Avignon in a painting by Ignazio Danti kept in the Geographic Maps Gallery, Vatican City.

33 top right The original copy of the Edict of Nantes (1598), which granted religious freedom to the Huguenots (Archives Nationales, Paris).

34 top In the 18th
century the city and
port of Toulon were
expanding rapidly;
the local shipyard,
enlarged by Colbert
in 1664, was the
strategic center of
the French Navy.
This painting by
Claude Joseph
Vernet is in the
Louvre, Paris.

34-35 The port of
Marseilles in 1666,
with the shipyard
where the best ships
in France were

built. After
conquering the city,
Louis XIV set out to
make it the gate to
the Mediterranean
and decided to
enlarge it.

35 top This
painting by Gordot
(Musée Calvet,
Avignon) represents
the entrance of the
Pope's vice legate
into Avignon,
performed with
great pomp, as was
the custom in that
period.

Yet the rebellious spirit of Provence
continued to bother the French
crown which was anxious to establish
total power over all of the country. In
1664, Louis XIV put a Parisian inten-
dant in charge of the parliament in
Aix who was entrusted with dealing
with questions of rights, security and
finance. The state lackeys, who continued to be sent until the end of the
18th century, fell in love with the region and made Aix into a rich and
important city with roads and luxurious houses.

Only Marseilles continued to wor-

ry Louis XIV until, out of patience, he
had the city walls breached on March
2, 1660 in a threat of violence to
show that all opposition was useless.

The offence caused to Marseilles
was repaid by the finance minister,
Colbert, who, hoping to increase the
state economy, made Marseilles a free
port in 1669 so greatly increasing
trade. The minister's edict exempted
goods arriving from the East from
the 20 percent tax that other ports
were obliged to pay. As Colbert had
forecast, Marseilles became an obligatory stop for goods on their way to

the Caribbean and was able to gain an ever larger foothold in the East where the city sold sugar and coffee from the Antilles. While the port of Marseilles was dedicated to trade, nearby Toulon, where Henri IV had created an arms depot, became the heart of the French navy.

The end of the 17th century saw the creation of a business in the region that is still highly active: the first *Faïenceries* (potteries) were built at Moustiers and Saint-Jean-du-

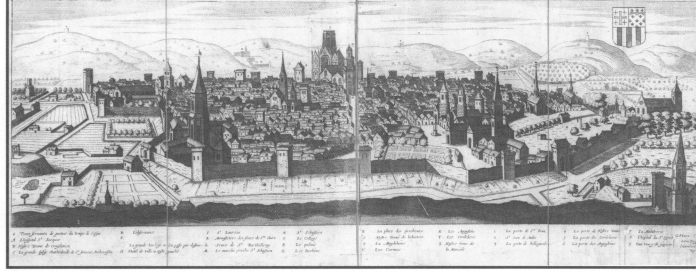

Désert near Marseilles. Initially, manufacture was an extremely simple procedure with the objects then being painted and fired, but firing techniques were perfected in the 18th and 19th centuries by craftsmen who turned out small works of art which are today considered highly desirable objects.

The plague that affected the region for years struck the city particularly hard in 1720 but Marseilles still managed to maintain its role of a rich and commercial city.

35 center
The old map of Aix-en-Provence in the Civic Museum of Arbaud shows the city surrounded by walls. In the middle is the grandiose Saint-Sauveur Cathedral.

35 bottom Michel Serre's Marseilles During the 1720 Plague *bears witness to the devastation wrought by the epidemic in the city.*

The rebel soul of Marseilles showed itself once more with the French Revolution. In 1792, the city sent "missionaries of patriotism" into the deepest countryside with the aim of spreading revolutionary principles. A battalion of more than five hundred volunteer soldiers set off for Paris the same year to support their compatriots in the struggle against the foreign supporters of Louis XVI. To pay tribute to the courage and enthusiasm of the revolutionaries, Rouget de Lisle composed the song of war that has since become the country's national anthem, the "Marseillaise."

The years that followed were characterized by bloody conflict and struggles between the Jacobins and the Royalists. The region remained unquiet and not even Napoleon succeeded in making himself appreciated as the Provençals blamed him for the economic blockade that damaged trade and industry. The region did not flourish again until 1830 with the July monarchy. As a result of the conquest of Algeria, Marseilles became one of France's most important ports and assumed

36 bottom In 1790-91 Avignon was the theater of bloody battles between French patriots and papists. The annexation of the city was sanctioned constitutionally in 1791 and ratified by the National Convention in 1793, but it was accepted by the Papal See only in 1814.

37 top The Marseillaise was the battle song of the Rhine army, which took in thousands of volunteers from all parts of France to support the revolutionary cause.

37 center Napoleon III was accepted grudgingly by the people of Provence. When he ascended the throne in 1851, eastern Provence became one of the centers of resistance against the emperor, who defeated the republicans at Mées.

37 bottom This 1835 print after a drawing by T. Allom shows the Triumphal Arch of Marseilles.

36-37 In 1792 Rouget de l'Isle wrote the Marseillaise, which later became the French national anthem. This composition was written to accompany the battalion of over five hundred volunteers who went north to help the revolutionaries in their struggle against the supporters of Louis XVI.

major significance during the industrial revolution with production of Marseilles soap, oil pressing and ship building. The arsenal at Toulon that employed thousands of people increased in size and became a model city.

With the end of the July monarchy in 1848, Provence once more expressed its hostility to the Bonapartists with its institution of universal suffrage, and when in December 1851 Louis Napoleon Bonaparte seized power, eastern Provence became one of the centers of resistance against the emperor. Consequently Napoleon was forced to send troops that same month to defeat the Republicans at Mées.

38 top In 1879 the Marseillais Clovis Hugues was elected to Parliament, becoming the first socialist deputy in French history.

38 center The Russian troops that landed at Marseilles in 1916 march through the Canebière. The First World War triggered a serious crisis in Provence.

38 bottom German troops enter Marseilles in 1942 through the Triumphal Arch. The following year they destroyed the Vieux-Port quarter, which they considered a hideout for Jews and Resistance fighters. The German occupation lasted almost two years, up to 1944.

Following its opposition to Napoleon III, Marseilles offered unconditional support to the Third Republic (1870-1940) and became a stronghold of socialism. The first congress of the Workers' Party took place here in 1879 and the city sent Clovis Hugues, the first Socialist deputy in history, to the Paris parliament.

Marseilles developed into one of the world's most important commercial ports at the outbreak of World War I, both for goods and for the passengers that set sail for the country's African colonies.

World War II brought a great blow to the industries of Provence. In 1940, France was cut in two with the Germans occupying the Atlantic coast; political refugees from all

around Europe converged on Marseilles, the country's single large unoccupied port, with the hope of sailing from there to the Unites States. Among these were the group of Surrealist painters headed by André Breton and Max Ernst to whom Peggy Guggenheim made a sea-plane available to leave the city. Being a strategic means of passage between the north and south, the region was occupied by the Italians in 1942 and then by the Germans who bombarded the port of Toulon. Marseilles suffered the same treatment but, rebellious as ever, refused to surrender. A Resistance group was created in the city, which was implacably persecuted by the Germans.

38-39 *August 15,*
1944: the Allied army
lands in Provence.
Most of the battles
took place in Toulon
and Marseilles, and
the Germans
surrendered after
having destroyed the
port areas.

39 *bottom left*
On November 11,
1942 the German
troops invaded
Southern France. Two
weeks later, the French
Navy sank its ships
at Toulon rather than
hand them over to
the enemy.

39 *bottom right*
On July 29, 1944
young women marched
through the streets of
Marseilles acclaiming
the Liberation. The
German occupation
was considered a
catastrophe for the
port city.

The landing of the Allies on the Mediterranean coast on August 15, 1944 marked the liberation of Provence from the Germans. After the end of the war, tourism took hold in the region, both on the coast and inland. As for Marseilles, large petroleum refineries and petrochemical industries sprang up around Etang de Berre and Fons but the damage caused to the port during the war had major repercussions on the city's economy for a long time.

After the glories of Nice, the cinema discovered the enchanting attractions of Saint-Tropez with its narrow, tightly squeezed ochre houses that overlook the ancient port. In 1955, Brigitte Bardot made her film debut here as the main character in the film *Et Dieu Créa la Femme* with her husband Roger Vadim. She built the famous villa *Madrague* where she hides away as soon as her commitments permit her. Intellectuals prefer the ancient villages hidden among the olive trees. Jean Giono praised the charm of Manosque in his novels and the poet René Char settled at Isle-sur-la-Sorgue. Though Saint-Paul de Vence is one of the prime tourist attractions inland, there is no longer any isolated village that has kept its secrets hidden. Ménerbes, Sault, Roussillon and Lourmarin are all villages that have had their old houses rebuilt with taste where famous people, such as Jacques Chirac, come to enjoy the atmosphere that has captivated artists from around

40 bottom In the 1960s Saint-Tropez was the scene of the romance between Jane Fonda and Roger Vadim. When she returned to the United States after her stay in France, Fonda declared that Vadim was a marvelous person.

40-41 During the day, the lively crowd at Saint-Tropez frequents the Crêperie at the port, and in the evening goes to the Pirate, a haunt of actors, film-makers and the international jet set.

41 bottom Saint-Tropez is the undisputed domain of Brigitte Bardot, who made her debut here in the film Et Dieu Créa la Femme. The actress likes to spend her vacation in her villa, La Madrague.

the world for centuries.

The vocation of modern Provence, which makes up part of the region Alpes-Provence-Côte d'Azur, is unquestionably tourism. This has brought exploitation and investment in, not just coastal tourist facilities, but also ancient inland villages as the authorities attempt to preserve the traditional features of this wonderful land. The summer festivals, like those at Avignon and *Chorégies* in Orange, are known around the world as major attractions to the modern traveler.

40 top The love story between Yves Montand and Simone Signoret began in the romantic setting of Saint-Paul-de-Vence. The two actors met at the the famous Colombe d'Or restaurant, which now has a fine collection of works left by artists to pay their bills.

profile bust facing the viewer's right, depicting a thoughtful, severe Van Gogh. He dedicated the work to his friend Laval (lower right-hand corner).

One gets the impression that the artist is looking into the mirror without seeing himself, absorbed as he is in his thoughts, which remove him from reality.

*42 top right
In* The Sower, *which he painted in June 1888, Van Gogh celebrates rural serenity and the splendor of the sun. The work betrays a peaceful state of mind.*

A cobalt blue sky, bright sunshine, gentle hills, bare mountains, stately rivers, cliffs that rise vertically from the blue sea where "the boats rise and fall" like doves, as Paul Valèry wrote: this is the Provence loved by artists.

Van Gogh arrived in 1888 to glorify these places in his inimitable manner and with a magical evocative force. First, he stayed at the Carrel restaurant in Arles, then he rented a house in the huge Place Lamartine (that has since become famous as

*42 center right
Van Gogh painted this landscape in May 1888. The artist was fascinated by the environs of Arles: in this work he painted the fields of irises, in the foreground, with the distant town in the background.*

*42 bottom right
There are at least five canvases of Van Gogh's bedroom at Arles. The one reproduced here with an intimate tone, was painted in September 1889 and gives the impression of a room that has been lived in, imbued with the artist's presence.*

43 L'Arlésienne *is the second of the six portraits Van Gogh did of Madame Ginoux. In this painting, characterized by strong contrasting colors, the woman seems severe, her face hardened much like a stone sculpture.*

44-45 Cézanne considered Mount Sainte-Victoire the symbol of Aix-en-Provence and of the land where he was born, and continued to paint it till he died. But he never called it by name, since no one could mistake it, merely writing "viewed from southwest," "from the south," and so on. This was the mountain par excellence, painted with strong brushwork and joyous colors. This work, now in the Hermitage, St. Petersburg, imparts the joy of living in this blessed land.

44 bottom Les Grandes Baigneuses, one of Paul Cézanne's most famous works, is kept in the Musée Granet, Aix-en-Provence. He painted it in his studio in the town center, which is now open to the public.

*45 bottom left
Maurice Denis, one
of the first artists and
critics who
appreciated Cézanne,
executed this work,
Paying a Visit to
Cézanne, as a tribute
to his friend. The sky
is typically Provençal,
and the hills and
vegetation are
suffused in a light
that seems to radiate
an opalescent powder.
Denis' art, which has
Neo-Classic
overtones, is quite
distant from
Cézanne's
substantial forms.*

*45 top right
Cézanne painted
many self-portraits.
He loved to depict his
various severe facial
expressions, which at
times he rendered
more detached
by wearing a
bowler hat.*

*45 top left The
Estaque, the Gulf of
Marseilles, is a motif
that Cézanne painted
several times and that
Braque and Picasso
also liked. Cézanne's
Estaque, which
anticipated many
modern artists, has
been viewed as a
revolutionary work, a
new way of painting,
in small cubes.*

"the yellow house") where he wanted to create a studio for artists: L'atelier du Midi. The first painter to accept his invitation was Gauguin but he did not share Van Gogh's love for Provence to the extent that the two quarreled and separated. On his first arrival in Arles, Van Gogh had been enthused by the explosion of blooms in March and painted as though he found himself in a "Provençal Japan." He painted intensely by both day and night: corn fields, almond trees in blossom, flights of crows, sunflowers, tragic skies, the interiors of houses, squares, portraits, and bridges around Arles similar in composition to Japanese landscapes. The best known of these is *Langlois Bridge* which had attracted him from his arrival. The painter also loved to depict the lights and shadows of night. He would stand at his easel, wearing a broad-brimmed hat on which he had at-

tached candles to throw light onto his palette and canvas. This was how he painted the *Café at Night*. Thirsty for life, for friendship and for the desire to reveal the secret of everything, yet in a constant struggle with himself and tormented by the continual sensation that evil had triumphed over good in the world, he continued until he ended in the psychiatric hospital at Saint-Paul-de-Mausole near Saint-Rémy in 1889, the year before he died and the year before Toulouse Lautrec challenged his friend, painter Henry de Groux, to a duel in response to a denigrating comment made about one of his pictures.

Nor could the painter Paul Cézanne stay away from his birthplace, Aix-en-Provence, for long even if his dissension with his father – who had changed profession from a hatter to a banker and did not like his son's choice – was never resolved. While living in Paris, Cézanne felt physically drawn back to the people and countryside of Mont Sainte-Victoire, which he painted time and again with ceaseless love. He stood at the window of Jas de Bouffan, bought by his father in 1859, and painted the land: the caves of Bibémus that fascinated him for their uninterrupted sequence of geometric shapes, the cubes of the houses, the rocks in the mountains, the farms and the flowers. After the death of his beloved mother, he built

loveliest museums, dedicated to this artist.

Picasso passed several years working in Antibes, close to Biot, and, a little farther away at Vallauris, in 1950 he founded one of France's most important centers for ceramic art with Madoura and Prinnier. His liking for Provence prompted him in 1958 to buy the castle of Vauvenargues that stands in front of Mont Sainte-Victoire near Aix where he worked until 1961. He left the castle to move to Mougins, a few miles north of Cannes, where he died in 1973 but he wanted to be buried in the grounds of the castle in front of the symbol of the *dominus*, in front of the mountain celebrated by Cèzanne, in front of the queen of Provence.

a studio at Chemin des Lauves (today Avenue Paul Cèzanne) in which he never ceased to paint his favorite mountain. He would begin at dawn to capture its awakening, its first breath and its sense of dominion over the whole region. While at Pont-des-Trois Sautets near Aix-en-Provence during the seven-year period from 1898 to 1905, Cézanne painted one of his masterpieces, *Les Grandes Baigneuses*, which inspired *Les Demoiselles d'Avignon* by Picasso in 1907, considered the manifesto of Cubism.

All painters felt at home in Provence. Not even Claude Monet, who in 1872 in his native Le Havre had painted the famous *Impression. Sunrise*, from which the name Impressionism was taken, and loved the cerulean sea of the north and its tempestuous sky, was able to resist the charms of Provence and spent an intense period near Marseilles in 1883 and another in Antibes in 1888.

Matisse and Bonnard moved permanently to Saint-Tropez. Fernand Léger, whose paintings illustrated the dynamism of modern life, established himself at Biot in a studio with an earthen floor, as was common in the houses of farmworkers, and today the village is home to one of France's

46-47 In 1889 Renoir wanted to paint Cézanne's beloved mountain, Sainte-Victoire, in his own way. As we can see, the celebration of the mountain is secondary compared to the triumphal blaze of colors, with the setting sun imparting a soft light onto the surrounding countryside.

MARSEILLE,
GATEWAY TO THE EAST

*49 top right
Off the coast of
Marseilles is the
Château d'If, the
tiny cliff-like island
with the castle-prison
that was the setting
for part of Alexandre
Dumas'* Count of
Montecristo.

48 Notre-Dame-de-la-Garde, the "Good Mother" as the Marseillais like to call this church, dominates the city. On the top of this gigantic Neo-Byzantine construction designed in the 19th century by the architect Espérandieu, is the monumental statue of the Virgin and Child. On Ascension Day the church is visited by sailors who make a pilgrimage there and offer ex-votos to the Virgin.

48-49 and 49 top left Opening out to the south onto the large Gulf of the Lion and delimited to the northeast by the Provençal Alps, its sky cleared of clouds by the mistral, Marseilles seems to hug the old port between the red walls of the Saint-Jean and Saint-Nicolas forts. Among the few buildings of the old quarter around the port, which was destroyed by the Germans in 1943, is the 17th century Hôtel de Ville, or town hall. The old port is now a huge parking space for sailboats and motorboats.

"Construction and destruction follow one another without cease. No era, no power and no concept is eternal here..." This was how, in 1925, Joseph Roth described the character of the city that is today the capital of the region in his book *The White Cities* after a long trip in the south of France. Very different from other Provençal cities like Arles or Aix, where shady squares and centuries-old streets were built on a human scale, Marseilles, wrapped in the blue of the sea and the white of limestone rocks, is in continual evolution. The "Gateway to the East," in which Greeks, Romans, Jews, French, Lebanese, Italians and natives of the Maghreb have mixed over the centuries, has always been a crossroads of civilizations and still produces surprising contrasts. Officially, North Africans number only 10 percent of the population of 800,000 but in some streets one breaths the atmosphere of the medina, for example, Cours Belsunce where *kaftan* and *tchador* can be glimpsed through the windows.

From whatever direction one arrives in Marseilles, the first view of the city is of Notre-Dame-de-la-Garde. La Bonne Mère, as it is affectionately called by the Marseillais, dominates the city. From its heights, one can see the spectacular *calanques*, inlets surrounded by striking rocky cliffs, and the natural curve of the old port flanked by the forts of St. Jean and St. Nicolas that were built by Louis XIV, not to protect the city but to intimi-

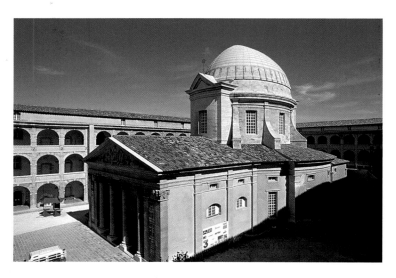

50 top left
In the old Panier quarter is the Vieille Charité, the hospice built in the second half of the 17th century by Louis XIV and now perfectly restored. The pink stone building with three tiers of galleries surrounded the Chapelle de la Charité, a Baroque masterpiece by the architect Pierre Puget.

50 top right
Discovering
Marseilles also
involves discovering
its museums. The
Palais Longchamp,
a Neo-Baroque
building designed by
Henri Espérandieu
in 1862-69, is the
home of the Natural
History Museum,
the Art Museum
and the
Numismatic
Collection.

50-51 The old Notre-
Dame-de-la-Major
cathedral, most of
which was disfigured
by the mid-19th
century construction
of the Nouvelle
Major, is the oldest
church in Marseilles.
It was built in 381,
destroyed centuries
later by the Saracens,
and then rebuilt in
the 1800s.

51 top left and right
The old cathedral
originally consisted of
several superposed
churches and a
baptistery. Today the
only remains are an
11th century apse,
one of the five
original spans of the
nave and one of those
in the 12th century
aisles. The rest was
razed to the ground
in 1852 to make
room for the present-
day Neo-Byzantine

date it. Further north, are the artificial basins of the Joliette and the outline of the small port of Estaque; this was one of Braque's favorite subjects, which he painted for the particular luminosity of the scenery. A little out to sea stands the Chateau d'If made famous by Alexandre Dumas in his novel, *The Count of Montecristo*. In the little port, where the houses were nearly all rebuilt after World War II, a forest of masts appears to grow from the sea and one senses the atmosphere of long trips and far away lands. Each morning, the crews chatter briskly in their strong Marseillais accent as the colored fishing boats return to the quay bearing tuna, sea bass, sea bream, shrimp and scorpion fish. It is the women who are responsible for selling them: wives, mothers and sisters, all strong and well-suited to commerce. In front of the Vieux Port stretches the long and busy Canebière, a street with an incredible number of shops, that takes its name from an old hemp rope-factory. The street is so famous that it was featured in the films and comedies of Marcel Pagnol who based his works on life in Marseilles during the 1920s.

Walking through the city, one realizes that something is changing. *Marseille ça bouge*, Marseilles is moving, someone says, and as it renews itself, it refinds its past. In the old district of Panier, La Vieille Charité, the hospice built during the second half of the 17th century by Louis XIV around the lovely Baroque Chapelle de la Charité designed by Pierre Puget, has been perfectly rebuilt and is now home to a lively cultural center. It stands in the heart of old Marseilles, a maze of dark, narrow streets on the Montée des Accoules which was featured in famous films like *Borsalino* and *The French Connection*. The times of organized crime seem a distant memory now that the city is rebuilding its older districts, creating pedestrian precincts like Rue Saint Ferréol, and replastering old façades. Right in the center, the Cours Estienne d'Orvres had fallen to the level of a parking lot but, today, that has been placed underground and the square has now been given a facelift with fashionable bistros and a charming bookshop whose name, *Les Arcenaulx*, is a reminder of the time when this area used to be a dockyard in which Charles VIII built the ships he sent down to Italy.

Whereas Notre-Dame-de-la-Garde embraces the city from above, the *tour de la corniche* encompasses it from the coast. The *corniche* is the long walkway along the seafront that connects the city to the vallon des Auffes built in 1863. Above the *corniche*, the colline du Roucas-Blanc where luxurious villas were built during the second half of the 19th century recalls a happy period for the city, when the "Porte d'Orient" grew wealthier after the opening of the Suez canal. Examples are the sumptuous Villa Valmer, the Petit Nice, the Talabot castle with its splendid park, and the Borély castle built by the magnate Louis Borély.

cathedral, under
which is the
octagonal baptistery
built around 381.
Inside are a 15th
century ceramic bas-
relief attributed to
the Della Robbia
and the marble St.
Lazarus altarpiece,
a work by Francesco
Laurana executed in
1480.

AVIGNON, PAPAL DRAMA

52 top In the heart of Avignon is the Place de l'Horloge, with the theater and town hall.

*52 center
The impressive Saint-André fort, built in the 14th century to keep guard over Avignon and protect its bridge.*

52 bottom Not far from Avignon, the Pont du Gard was a fundamental link in the aqueduct that channeled water to the fountains in Nîmes. Built 2000 years ago, this aqueduct is one of the greatest achievements of Roman engineering and is still perfectly intact.

52-53 and 53 top right Surrounded by 14th century walls and washed by the Rhône river on two sides, Avignon was a mere village in the 1200s and became a prosperous city with impressive palaces, towers and bell-towers when the popes used it as the papal residence from 1309 to 1377.

*53 top left
The famous Avignon bridge is really called Pont Saint-Bénézet, named after the shepherd who, inspired by a divine voice, had it built in 1177. The bridge was destroyed and rebuilt several times, until floods in the 1600s reduced it to its present state.*

As much as Marseilles is in the throes of change, the compact and harmonious city of Avignon seems to have been kept in a jewel case. Surrounded by a long rectangle of city walls and flanked on two sides by the river Rhône, the City of the Popes is an artistic and cultural pearl, a melting pot of flamboyant Gothic architecture. The golden age of Avignon coincided with the period of the popes' stay, from 1309 to 1377, when the papacy moved its seat to the Midi to avoid the political intrigues that took place in Rome. The result was the construction of a new city with palaces, towers, bell-towers and churches but it was the popes' palace that made Avignon unique. The building of the Palais Vieux with its four imposing and austere corner towers began in 1336 when Pope Benedict XII, the third Avignon pope, ordered the demolition of the old bishop's palace that his predecessor, John XXII, had only just had enlarged. The massive walls hid courtyards, enormous salons and unending suites of rooms. Benedict's successor, Clement VI, had the palace doubled in size and called a troupe of Italian artists headed by Simone Martini and, later, Matteo Giovanetti to his court, who decorated it with such magnificence that it appeared to want to outdo the pomp of the Roman court. This was how the Palais Neuf came into being, a combination of castle, court and fortress with ten large towers to protect it

from unexpected attack. The main court, the 19,375 square feet *cours d'honneur*, opens majestically just inside the entrance; this is the site of the Theater Festival, begun in 1947 by Jean Vilar, which still continues to this day with great success.

However, the Popes' Palace is not the only architectural work of art in Avignon. Overlooking the Place du Palais is the 12th century cathedral of Notre-Dames-des-Doms that was once decorated with splendid frescoes now preserved in the Palace, and the 14th century Petit Palais which houses an interesting museum. Its rooms are nearly all dedicated to Italian art apart from the last three, which deal with painting and sculpture from Avignon.

The city is especially enjoyable on foot at sunset when the weak light of the sun reflects off its cream-colored stone. Every corner has curiosities to be discovered, beginning with the Balance district, the ancient gypsy quarter, where restored Gothic palazzi and modern Mediterranean style houses are well blended into the architecture of the past. Centuries ago, King René also fell in love with this city and had a house built here in Rue de Grivolas. The King came here when he preferred a little peace to the luxury and vivacity of the court of Aix or the castle in Tarascon.

56 top left
The wide, tree-lined
17th century Cours
Mirabeau, named
after the fiery deputy
of the Revolution in
the 19th century, was
once reserved for
carriage rides. The
locals still love to walk
in the shade of the
plane trees and sit
in the outdoor cafés
to watch the world
pass by.

56 top right
At the Rotunda, at
the beginning of
Cours Mirabeau,
there is a refreshing
fountain decorated
with lions and sea
lions, built during
Napoleon III's reign,
that is a spectacular
sight indeed.

AIX-EN-PROVENCE, THE CITY OF FOUNTAINS

Aix, the city of "Good King" René, ancient capital of Provence and homeland of Paul Cèzanne and Count Mirabeau – unyielding representative of the Third Estate during the French revolution – greets the visitor with its many fountains, lovely tree-lined streets and elegant Renaissance and Baroque palaces. Its mild climate enchanted the counts of Provence and the strict financial intendants of Louis XIV who contributed to making it yet lovelier and richer. Reminders of Cèzanne, who spent much of his life in Aix fascinated by the light and colors of the surrounding countryside, are all around the city. A sign-posted route around the city streets takes the visitor to the places where the artist lived: the Collège Mignet in Rue Cardinale where he became friends with Émile Zola, his drawing school next to the Granet museum, the house where he was born and, a few hundred yards from the cathedral, his workshop where he painted one of his most famous paintings, *Les Grandes Baigneuses*.

To its other great citizen, Mirabeau, Aix has dedicated the boulevard that bears his name. The long, wide avenue is shaded by huge plane trees and lined by magnificent palaces that alternate classical simplicity with the ornateness of the Baroque. It is an ideal place to relax, seated in one of its many cafés, like the Café des Garçons where Cèzanne liked to *regarder passer le temps*, watch time pass by.

56-57 The former capital of Provence, Aix-en-Provence, the city of the "Good King" René, Mirabeau and Cézanne, owes its name to the Roman consul Sextius, who in 123 BC set up camp with his troops at the thermal springs.

*57 top left
Aix is also known as "the city of fountains," as can be seen in this photograph of a detail of the fountain with statues of four dolphins.*

*57 top right
In the old Saint-Sauveur quarter is the cathedral of the same name, built in the fifth century and rebuilt several times up to the 18th century. It conceals a Romanesque cloister with thin columns whose capitals have floral motifs.*

57 center right and bottom The flamboyant Gothic façade of the cathedral is decorated with elegant pinnacles and statues. In the interior is the famous triptych of the Burning Bush by Nicolas Froment, as well as splendid Flemish tapestries from the Canterbury Cathedral that decorate the choir.

The oldest section of the city is San Salvatore, which stands on the ruins of the imperial city founded by the Romans. It rings the university and the cathedral of San Salvatore that was begun in the fifth century and only completed thirteen hundred years later. The façade, like the rest of the cathedral, shows signs of many architectural styles: Provençal Romanesque, Gothic and flamboyant Gothic reveal the periods during which the building was renovated. Snaking around the cathedral are the old streets of the district, like Rue Gaston Saporta, one of the most elegant with antique and craft shops and aristocratic houses adorned with decorations and columns. A short distance from Saint-Saveur stands the Pavillon de Vendôme, built in the 17th century on land given by Provence to Duke Louis de Vendôme, nephew of Henri IV, for having contributed to the pacification of the region. Facing onto a small French garden, the pavillon today houses a delightful museum dedicated to the life of Provence with portraits of the most important figures in the history of Aix, a series of still-lifes and some attractive majolicas from Moustiers.

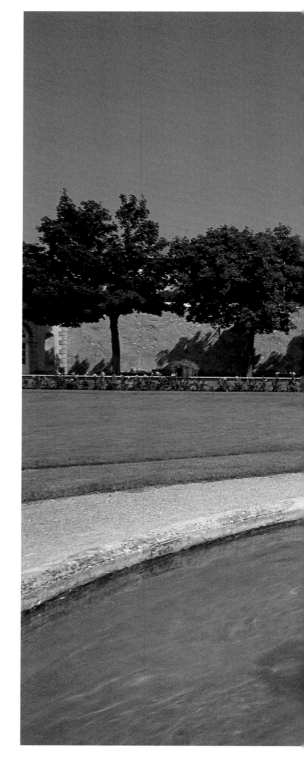

ORANGE, A THEATER FOR ETERNITY

60 top left and top right The Roman theater in Orange, dating from the first century AD, has a stage wall that is so fascinting that Louis XIV called it "the most beautiful wall in my kingdom." The

Romans used the slope of the Saint-Europe hill to build the tiers, which are still intact. The entrance, blind arches, and rows of Corinthian columns are perfectly preserved.

The entrance to the city of Orange from the north offers a majestic welcome through its triumphal Roman arch, the symbolic gateway to Provence, which was built in 20 BC on the ancient Via Agrippa that connected Lyons to Arles. It is seventy-one feet tall with three arcades framed by beautiful

columns, an elegant pediment and two attics, one on top of the other, and is considered one of the loveliest triumphal arches from the Roman era. Bas-reliefs filled with movement and character depict the pacification of Gaul and the victories of Augustus. Founded by the Latin civilization around 35 BC, Orange was a principality belonging to the duchy of Nassau from the 16th century until the Treaty of Utrecht in 1713 when it was returned to France. In addition to the arch, the city is even prouder of its ancient Theater in which the 335 foot long and 120 foot high stage wall still stands: "The most beautiful wall in my kingdom," Louis XIV used to say. The superb construction was built during the reign of Augustus in the lee of a hill as the setting for all kinds of performances: plays, dancing, singing and festivals. The quality of its acoustics and the excellent state of preservation make it the foremost theater remaining from the Roman era. These qualities mean that the theater is still used for public performances of the internationally famous series of operas and musical shows named *Chorégies*. The center of the small city lies a few minutes walk away where its heart, the lovely Place Clemenceau, is overlooked by fine town houses with decorated façades.

60 bottom left The powerful statue of Augustus greeting the audience stands in a niche in the stage wall of the ancient theater.

60 center right Built on the ancient Via Agrippa that connected Lyons and Arles, the triumphal arch in Orange was the first Roman monument in Gaul, and symbolized the power of Rome. Recent research has dated it back to around 20 BC. Fifty years later it was named after the emperor Tiberius.

60 bottom right The triumphal arch is seventy-two feet high and is well preserved, with obvious restoration work on the western side. It has three arches framed by lovely columns and a pediment decorated with low-reliefs depicting scenes of battles between the Romans and Celts.

61 The city of Orange, which has important vestiges of the past, is a must for opera lovers as well. Every year the Chorégies festival features the greatest interpeters of Verdi and Wagner in the ancient theater.

ARLES, ART AND BULLFIGHTS

O f all the cities in Provence, the most lively is Arles, a true hotbed of initiatives. The Romans were appreciative of its success in commerce and in its ability to establish relations with the whole of the known world of the time. It flourished to the point that everything that civilization had to offer in terms of foodstuffs, fabrics, precious objects, bronze, copper etc. could be found there. Arles was the favorite city of Vincent Van Gogh and where he found inspiration for his paintings of sparkling fields of sunflowers in the surrounding country-

side. Nowadays, it never ceases to amaze for its variety of gatherings and festivals: concerts, shows, bull-fights, the rice festival, an international salon for the *Santonniers* (the sculptors of the figures in representations of the Holy Manger), the festival of the *gardians* of the Camargue, and international photographic meetings that brought the national school of photography into being. Facing onto the Rhône and flooded by the vibrant light of Provence that has proved so popular with painters and poets, the city, wrapped in the strong colors of the surrounding country, continues to inspire every form of creativity; for example, the clothes designer from Arles, Christian Lacroix, used the glittering costumes of the toreadors and the traditional clothes of the women as the inspiration for the collections which made him famous around the world. One comes to Arles to know a city that has a rich artistic and historical tradition into which the Roman remains blend perfectly. Its past continues to live in its ancient monuments: the arena – today used for bull-fights – and the medieval fortified bastion built to defend the city against the raids of the Saracens. From the top of the entrance tower, one's gaze takes in the Romanesque abbey of Montmajour three miles away on a hilltop shaded by pines where Van Gogh often used to paint. Next to the arena stands the theater built in 30 BC framed by large trees that act as a backdrop to the Romanesque bell-tower of Saint-Trophime. Then there are Constantine's baths and the austere parade of sar-

63

cophagi of the Alyscamps, the famous Roman and paleo-Christian necropolis. Five years ago, the superb Musée de l'Arles Antique was built in the same place that the immense first century AD Roman circus used to stand on the right bank of the Rhône. It was designed by Henri Cipriani in the shape of a triangle whose sides correspond to the three sections of the museum and is as blue as the Provençal sky. The first side is dedicated to archaeology and contains a spectacular model of how the city used to be during the Roman era; the second houses the museum's scientific activities with a research section and laboratories for the restoration of ceramics and glass; the third is a welcome and information center for the public containing an extensive document center. Now, as in the past, the center of Arles is the Forum square, built on U-shaped crypto-porticoes – grandiose underground galleries – built by the Romans for storing grain and still in fine condition. Looking onto the square is the famous Hôtel Nord-Pinus, described by Jean Cocteau, who used to stay there, as a hotel with a soul. And a lively soul it is too, reflecting the personalities of its past owners, the tight-rope walker of the Medrano circus, Nello Bessières, and his wife Germaine, a fiery cabaret dancer, who was a great friend of Edith Piaf. Its guest book contains signatures of some of the great figures of the century: Winston Churchill, Sacha Guitry, King Farouk, Jean-Paul Sartre, Paul Klee and Picasso. On the balcony of room ten, reserved for great toreadors, Luis Dominguin received the ovation of the crowd after a performance in the ring. Lining the walls of the Cintra bar at the Nord-Pinus are bull-fighting posters and photographs of toreadors in glittering costumes and of regular guests at the hotel, such as Yves Montand, Simone Signoret and Picasso in his favorite blue-lined sailor's sweater. Nowadays, the public crowds into the Forum square on bull-fight days and for three days they celebrate with *paella*, sherry and *flamenco* music. Emptied of the corrida crowd, the Forum square returns to being a calm, tranquil place where one goes to sit, in the shade of the huge plane trees protected by the statue of Frédérique Mistral, in the Café de la Nuit that was immortalized in a painting by Vincent Van Gogh and rebuilt a few years ago in the colors that dominate the picture: yellow, green and blue. Van Gogh arrived in Arles in February 1888 and stayed until May of the following year. Reminders of the artist are to be found everywhere in the city although many of the places shown in his paintings no longer exist, for example, the Maison Jaune in Place Lamartine in the north of the city, the famous bridge in the painting *Pont Langlois avec ses Lavandières* was moved 850 yards during work on Arles canal, and the old Hotel Dieu, the hospital to which the artist was taken when he cut off his right ear after an argument with Gauguin, has been turned into the Espace Van Gogh that houses a large library and display area.

66 top left and 67 Saint-Trophime church was built in the 12th century of limestone and is a fabulous example of Provençal Romanesque architecture. The expressive sculptures on the portal illustrated passages from the Bible to the pilgrims on their way to Santiago de Compostella. The most interesting scenes are The Last Judgement, Adoration of the Magi *and* Massacre of the Innocents.

66 bottom left The Saint-Trophime cloister is a masterpiece for its balanced, proportioned volumes and the artistic quality of the sculpture pieces. Two sides are Romanesque, while the other two are Gothic, with ogee arches supported by slender double columns decorated with acanthus leaves and symbolic images.

66 top right Rounding off the decoration of the portal of Saint-Trophime are the statues of St. Peter, St. John, St. Trophime, St. James and St. Bartholomew.

66 center right The simple, austere interior of Saint-Trophime is one of the most fascinating in Provence. Filled with light from the tall windows, it is sixty-five feet high.

66 bottom right The interior of the Arles cathedral is particularly austere and draws inspiration from ancient motifs: the vault rests on cornices decorated with acanthus leaves, while the capitals and small columns were influenced by Byzantine architecture.

The Fondation Van Gogh, directed by Yolande Clergue, has also been established in Arles. It has its offices in the 18th century de Luppé palace opposite the arena. No paintings by Van Gogh are displayed but there are paintings and sculptures created in homage to the master by contemporary artists. The result is a marvelous variety of themes inspired by Van Gogh: the sculptor Cèsar has displayed an 18th century armchair wrapped in a fishing net, Francis Bacon produced an oil painting showing the shadow of Van Gogh as it appeared in a self-portrait walking through Tarascon, and Fernando Botero painted a picture of a gigantic straw seat with a typical pair of Van Gogh boots lying on it.

Different styles and epochs exist together in Arles. In Place de la République we see the contrast between the solemnity of the City Hall built during the second half of the 18th century by Jules Mansart, the Sun King's architect, and the stirring 12th century Romanesque church and cloister of Saint-Trophime, one of the most beautiful in Provence, that has two sides built in Romanesque style and the other two in Gothic. The outstanding sculptures that decorate the portal provided a lesson in biblical culture to the pilgrims on their way to St. James cathedral in Santiago de Compostella.

In contrast to Arles' cultural side, there is the bustle of the Saturday morning market on Boulevard des

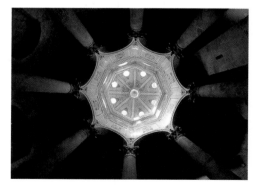

Lices, one of Provence's best. Typical are the stalls selling bull or donkey salami and goat cheese or mountains of fresh oysters and prawns. What makes this market different from others in France is the saddle-makers' section where the sale of bridles, stirrups, creams, boots and saddles remind us that Arles stands at the entrance to the Camargue, the kingdom of wild horses and the *gardians*.

TOULON, MARITIME TRADITIONS

Whereas the other cities of Provence have succeeded in maintaining their glorious heritage intact, Toulon suffered the ravages of World War II like no other. Today, the old city has lost its place to modern blocks with vividly colored windows but the invasion of cement has not succeeded in ruining the city's surrounding natural environment. The towers seem smaller from the *corniche* on Mont Faron that bristles with green cluster pines and the distant view stretches from the small and large docks as far as the Giens peninsula. To the traveler, modern Toulon still offers a magnificent setting: surrounded by green hills, it looks onto one of the most beautiful harbors in the Mediterranean, where Vauban, the great military architect of the Sun King, built the largest dockyard in the kingdom to outfit ships for the navy. It was here that on December 19, 1793 Napoleon showed his military genius for the first time when he stormed the city allied to the monarchist party and the English who were obliged to leave. The old dockyard, begun by Cardinal Richelieu and used as a port, has been conserved from Toulon's past while the new docks, built out of Vauban's project, are now a naval base.

ALONG THE COAST, FROM PORTS TO BAYS

71 top
Lying between Cavalaire and Le Lavandon, the Domaine du Rayol park is a magnificent oasis open to the public where an infinite number of endemic Mediterranean plants are grown. This botanic garden also has exotic plants and palms.

71 center
Carpeted by greenery, Cap Taillat juts out into the blue sea south of Saint-Tropez.

71 bottom
The white beach of Escalet, at Saint-Tropez, lies between the turquoise sea and the green maritime pines and maquis vegetation.

70 top left
Cap du Dramont, dominated by the Esterel cliff, softly descends to the sea opposite the Ile d'Or with its tall medieval tower.

70 top right
The craggy, barren coast of Marseilles, lashed by the mistral, which clears the sky, still has a wild look about it. Every day the old port is filled with fishermen who sell their catch early in the morning on the quay.

70-71 The rugged rocks of Esterel fall headlong into the sea in a phantasmagoria of color: from red to yellow to the purple of the lichens. All this is framed by islets and rocks, and coves and inlets create enchanting views.

An unbroken series of lighthouses, beaches and deep, well-protected bays with the occasional inlet so small that a sardine could block the entrance, as the Marseillais say. Off the coast lie islands where nature has been left untouched. Lining the seashore are cluster pines, palm trees and the Mediterranean maquis with its smells of rosemary, thyme, mastic tree and marjoram. The promontories on the coast – Cap du Pinet, Cap Camarat, Cap de l'Aigle – offer superb views of the sunrise and sunset. From the delta of the Rhône to the Esterel, the Provençal coast contains an incredible variety of landscapes and colors. In love with Saint-Tropez, Colette, the 20th century writer famous for her novels *Gigi and Claudine*, said, "The blue that rules the sky here is a color only dreamt of elsewhere, but on the Provençal riviera it arcs over everything." The sea too is a light, transparent blue which, at Saint-Tropez, washes up on the famous Pampelonne beach protected on one side by the lush and spectacular Cap Camarat and, on the other, by Cap Escalet. Here the cluster pines and vines grow right down to the beaches of golden sand separated by rocky points. The fame of Saint-Tropez, for many years nourished by the enthusiasm of Brigitte Bardot, has not diminished. During summer, tourists seated in the port cafés play the game of spotting the famous as they come ashore from their yachts moored in the harbor. Yet, even in the heart of the season, the *pétanque* players and lively, colorful market on Wednesdays and Saturdays in the Place des Lices, surrounded by centuries-old plane trees, seem a thousand miles away from the worldliness of the port. The view from the

citadel that guards the gulf covers the whole bay, from the massif des Maures to the Esterel that drops right down to the sea with its bare rock colored red and blue by porphyry and yellow and violet by lichen. The Annonciade Museum housed in an 18th century chapel next to the port holds paintings by such famous artists as Matisse, Derain, Braque and Dufy. Further back, the chapel of Saint Anne, protectress of the town, contains so many offerings that one might think it a small museum of the marina with its silhouettes and models of boats and drawings of the port. Built at an altitude of 675 feet to protect the area from the Saracens, the two villages Ramatuelle and Gassin are picturesque with narrow medieval streets lined with olive trees, eucalyptus and vines. They are ancient sentinels of the sea, like the lovely Grimaud that exudes the spirit of Provence and which is ennobled by Grimaldi castle with its three medieval towers and the small romantic church of Saint-Michel.

Although the peninsula of Saint-Tropez still boasts luxuriant vegetation, the road along the coastline between Cavalaire and Le Lavandou is lined by nothing but houses and hotels except for the botanical gardens named the Domaine du Rayol. They was created by a banker at the beginning of the 20th century to display thousands of plants that grow happily in the Mediterranean climate.

72 top
The regular hexagon of the citadel, with its three round towers and massive ramparts, reminds one of the war-like past of Saint-Tropez. From the top one can see the gulf, the Massif des Maures and the Esterel, as far as the Lérins islands and the offshoots of the Alps.

72 center
The tightly-packed ochre and pink houses with old tile roofs are a lovely background to the old port, which is always vivacious. The summer season opens with the Grand Prix off-shore race, while in August the town is one of the stages in the Tour de France for sailboats.

72 bottom Le Gorille is a must for anyone landing at Saint-Tropez. Along the quay are small restaurants and cafés that invite you to spend some time watching the sailboats and motorboats come and go.

72-73 The old port in Saint-Tropez is a favorite with those who have large yachts: the high life, small characteristic restaurants, and the chance to mingle with the international jet set, are an everlasting attraction.

73 top
The oldest houses in Saint-Tropez seem to rise up out of the sea, protected by the bell-tower of the church dedicated to the eponymic saint of the town, Saint-Tropez, who with sword and armor dominates the façade.

74 top In the midst of the green pine trees, the houses of the village of Porquerolles overlook the port: the village area features early 20th century villas that belonged to the owners of the island before the French Government purchased it in the 1970s, a wine-producing estate, bistros, and restaurants.

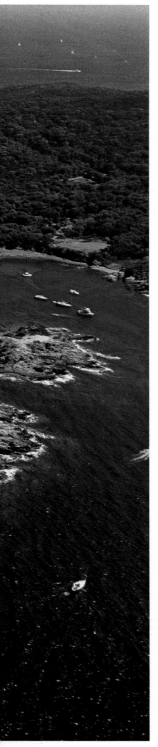

74-75 Opposite Hyères, the island of Porquerolles is a paradise for yachtsmen, who always find the right wind to hoist their sails and splendid coves to moor in. Deep inlets, sandy beaches and rocky coastlines are an ever-changing attraction for those spending a few days here.

75 top left The Petit Langoustier, situated north of the Grand Langoustier cape, looks like a rocky island with a fort, one of the many fortified constructions on the Hyères Islands that underscore the role of defensive outpost played by this archipelago.

75 top right The port of Porquerolles, sheltered from the formidable mistral, is a pleasant landing place for sailboats in all weather conditions. In high season it is impossible to find a berth if one does not book ahead months in advance.

Palm trees are an important feature of the landscape of Hyères, a small town reminiscent of the early 1900s and the oldest resort on the coast. It is the departure point for Hyères archipelago made up of three little islands with lush Provençal gardens, bearing the names Porquerolles, Port-Cros and l'Île du Levant. The three form a veritable oasis where nothing is lacking: in the center of Porquerolles there is a large, perfectly cultivated vineyard that produces a good rosé, which cheers the dining tables of the island. When pirates were at large in the area, they used the island as a refuge and the steps, now worn down by time and weather, that rise out of the sea at Porquerolles were used to carry booty from the boats up to the Pirates Gallery where it was hidden. The small port at Porquerolles filled with sailing boats is lined with houses colored a warm pink.

As always, the song of the cicadas, the smells of rosemary and the mastic trees, and the green of the tamarisks, eucalyptus and umbrella pines seduce anyone who sets foot on the island. The mainland is near but it seems part of another world; here everything is easier. The total absence of cars heightens this sensation – all travel is on foot or by bicycle. In the evening, when the bells fall quiet, silence reigns absolute and the magic of Porquerolles permeates the air even in high summer. Shaded paths and avenues bordered by immense pines with twisted roots invite the visitor to explore in search of charming beaches like the Plage de la Courtade or the Plage de Lequin to the right of the port, or small bays like l'Aiguade or steep rocks like the one that drops into the sea on Oustaou de Diou beach (ancient dialect for the House of God). Then there is the Plage d'Argent that takes its name from the color of the white quartz sand. And the Plage de Notre Dame on the other side of the village, perhaps the loveliest and most secluded of all, which Jean Luc Godard chose for scenes in his film Pierrot le Fou? The old Place des Armes is the center of life on the island where games of pétanque start each evening at sunset. Is that all there is? Anyone arriving from the mainland might think so at first but soon one realizes that the simplicity of this limited existence has its own fascination. It is easy to chat with the inhabitants of the island: just drop into the Bar de l'Escale for a pastis at aperitif time. This is an obligatory stop-off for the pétanque players as they each have a locker in which they keep their balls and the equally important duster to keep them clean.

75 bottom right The Mediterranean maquis, with its strong scent of rosemary and mastic, descends to the sea. The coast of the island was once a refuge for pirates, and visitors can still see the cave where they hid their treasures.

76 top Port-Cros, declared a national park, offers luxuriant nature with an infinite variety of plants and aromatic herbs that are protected by hard and fast regulations: it is forbidden to camp, light fires and even gather flowers on the island.

76 center The forts facing the sea are one of the features of the island of Port-Cros; in fact, there is a marked path along the coast so that visitors can discover them one by one. The 17th century Fort de l'Estissac, perhaps the loveliest, was partly rebuilt in 1793 and offers an enchanting panoramic view.

76 bottom The small bay of Port-Cros, sheltered to the west from the mistral by the islet of Bagaud, is truly out of this world. The village with its brightly colored houses along the inlet has about thirty inhabitants, but during the summer many tourists visit it.

76-77 Ile du Levant, the narrow, long island north-east of Port-Cros, has a rocky and almost inaccessible coastline. A small area is for nudists, while about 90 percent of the land is the property of the French Navy and is off-limits for the general public.

An hour away by boat lies the smaller island of Port-Cros, a national park, ringed by a glorious sea rich with fish of many different species. The village, arranged around a palm-lined avenue, is small enough to seem like Lilliput; the sea that crashes onto the jagged, rocky coast is a paradise for scuba divers. For those who love underwater exploration, the ideal scuba-diving attraction is a ship that sank at Port-Cros in 1968, which is now the habitat of colonies of sea-eels. Pines, olive trees and maquis with its huge variety of aromatic herbs grow wild inland. Even wilder is the island of the Levant, almost entirely owned by the French navy, just in front of Port-Cros. With its almost inaccessible cliffs, it is a paradise for nudists that arrive here every summer.

77 top left At the end of the Giens peninsula is the Tour-Fondue, the old redoubt built at the behest of Richelieu in 1634 that gave its name to the locality, which is the point of departure for ferries going to Porquerolles.

77 top right Port-Cros is truly a paradise for those who love scuba diving. Thanks to the laws forbidding fishing, the sea floor is filled with bass, gilthead, lobsters, shrimp and dassies. One of the attractions for divers is the wreck of a ship that sank here in 1968, which is the home of colonies of sea-eels.

79 top Cassis is one of the favorite haunts of the Marsellais. The piers of its port are the point of departure for boats going to the spectacular cliffs in the famous Calanques: Port-Pin, Port-Miou and En-Vau.

79 bottom Lying against the cliffs and hills is the lively town of Cassis, whose colorful houses face the charming fishermen's port. The town is famous for its shellfish accompanied by cassis, the dry, light liquor produced in this area.

78 top left Precipitous rocks overlooking the sea and blooming meadows are the features of the zone between Cassis and La Ciotat, the town that witnessed the birth of cinema. The coastline from the Camargue to the environs of Marseilles offers a panorama of uninterrupted beauty.

78 top right Celebrated by Mistral, the greatest Provençal poet, Cassis never stops amazing people with the variety of its landscape. The rocks on the western part of the bay are every bit as beautiful as the white cliffs of Dover.

78-79 The Cassis cliffs are one of the most spellbinding points of the Provençal coast. The rust-colored rock crowned with woods at Cap Canaille, which offer a magnificent view of the Puget massif and the islands, is in stark contrast with the blue sea, creating a play of colors that has inspired many modern painters.

The winds between the islands in the archipelago of Hyères make this an ideal area for sailing whereas the small port of Bandol on the far side of Toulon – with its fishing boats that arrive either early in the morning or at sunset and its promenade lined with palms and oleanders – is the resort for doing absolutely nothing. Around the village, magnificent vineyards have produced a red wine with a bouquet of vanilla and red fruits since ancient times. There is a strong temptation for the visitor to stop off in one of the many local taverns and sip at a glass of Provençal nectar. The Calanques, steep inlets created out of white limestone, drop into the emerald water between La Ciotat and Marseilles; these form one more spectacular feature among the many examples of natural splendor to be found in Provence. Confronted by such beauty, the enormous cranes in the dockyards at La Ciotat that seem to lift the entire port get forgotten. The name La Ciotat recalls the birth of cinema. Who could forget the first film of the Lumière brothers, *The Arrival of the Train at La Ciotat Station*, presented in Paris on December 28, 1895, that made the spectators at the Grand Café on Boulevard des Capucins jump out of their seats with amazement?

"If you've seen Paris but not seen Cassis, you haven't seen anything" is a local saying. The small town between La Ciotat and Marseilles overlooks a busy fishing port where fishermen unload their wares and has boutiques

dedicated to 19th century Provençal painting; the town's atmosphere is one of cheerfulness and *joie-de-vivre*. This is the departure point for sea trips to the nearby Calanques, a word that calls up thoughts of ancient geological epochs. The cleaves in the rocks extend for over one hundred yards below the water creating grottoes and an ideal habitat for fish. They were formed thousands of years ago by rivers rushing down to the sea which later rose and submerged them.

*80 top left and 80-81
The spectacle of the
Calanques in the
environs of Marseilles
is of incomparable
beauty: sheer rock
faces precipitating
into the sea, and
pinnacles that form a
barrier for delightful
inlets frequented
by sailboats and
fishing boats.*

The nearest to Cassis is Port-Miou ("safe refuge" in Provençal dialect) that runs inland for nearly a mile and is lined on either side by villas and gardens. Port-Pin is wilder, a half hour further on, with a well-protected, small stone beach and Aleppo pines clinging to the rock walls. At the marvelous En-Vau, where the perpendicular walls are used by rock climbers and a small beach is set between the rock pinnacles, the real Calanques scenery begins: the bright green of the vegetation, the dazzling white of the

*80 center left
Quite near the gullies
of Sormiou, in the
same massif, is the
Morgiou fjord. Here
rough trails offer
panoramic hikes, but
even from the sea the
view is superb. In July
and August this area
is inaccessible by land,
while in the other
months one can get
there by car.*

*80 bottom left
This tiny bay in the
middle of Calanques
and gorges is a ring
of rock surrounding
a body of water as
transparent as that
in a fountain.*

*80 right
The Calanques at
Sormiou are a
favorite haunt of the
Marsellais, who love
to clamber up the rock
faces of this fjord,
which are furrowed
by "trails" suitable
for all kinds and
levels of climbs.*

limestone, and the turquoise of the water. Then there are Sormiou and Morgiou with their *cabanons*, the small huts used by fishermen in the 19th century that have now been transformed into weekend retreats for Marseillais. At Cap Morgiou in 1985, a diver named Cosquer discovered a cave at the end of a tunnel 120 feet below the waterline. 20,000 years ago the cave would have been accessible on foot when it was decorated with wonderful wall paintings, interpreted as ritual signs of the hunt.

82 top The salt-pans in the Camargue at the borders of the Salin-de-Giraud east of the Grand Rhône, often take on a dreamlike aspect. Large, geometric evaporation basins, and hillocks and heaps of salt welcome the trucks used for transporting this product.

In direct contrast to the vertical Calanques, the horizontal stretch of the Camargue in the province of Arles is enclosed by the delta of the river Rhône. Here can be found salt flats, flower-covered meadows, rarely visited beaches and large lagoons around the Etang de Vaccarès, the home of flocks of flamingos. This is the French Wild West, the kingdom of the Camargue breed of horses, short-horned bulls raised for Spanish bull-rings and bulls with lyre-shaped horns used in the bullfights that take place in Arles. Overseeing all this are the *gardians*, heirs of ancient traditions, that ride horseback with a trident in hand. They are the custodians of the *manade*, which in Camargue means what you have in hand, i.e. hundreds of hectares of land that are home to animals free to wander and feed at will. Here and there stand the thatch-roofed *cabanes*, the low, oval, traditional white walled homes of the *gardians*. In the center of the *manade* stands the *mas*, the old patriarchal residence with wrought iron balconies. On either side of the property, unpaved roads hidden between the canes run alongside canals down to the huge white beaches where surfers and gourmets gather in the welcoming *cabanons* to eat fresh fish prepared by fishermen-cum-cooks.

84-85 and 84 top The Camargue lies between the mouths of the Petit Rhône and Grand Rhône: thousands of hectares of marshland populated by magnificent brightly-colored birds and vast prairies that are the domain of the famous horses and the bulls with lyre-shaped horns that are raised for the bloodless bullfights held at Arles. At Giraud the shallow seawater that penetrates the ponds evaporates from March to September, leaving a crust of salt about two inches high that is gathered from August to October.

85 top right
Excursions on horseback are one of the major attractions in the Camargue. This area offers riders the possibility to gallop through the immense prairies or follow paths along ponds and canals to observe the flight of numerous species of birds.

85 bottom right The Camargue horses are born black or grey and with time become white. They are small, very strong and wild. They are captured with lassos, branded and trained when they are three years old. Their job is to help the gardians lead the cattle.

85 top left The Camargue marshes are filled with fish. Covered by a cloud of seagulls, a fisherman hauls in his catch.

85 bottom left
On a green headland surrounded by swamps and prairies, is this cabane, a typical house for the gardians, the Camargue "cowboys." It is like a small chapel, low and oval to resist the strong wind, and has a thatched roof that touches the windows and walls.

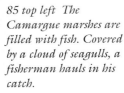

The best days in the Camargue are 24-25 May when the patron saint of gypsies, Saint Sarah, is commemorated at Saintes-Marie-de-la-Mer, by gypsies coming from all over Europe.

Saintes-Marie-de-la-Mer is now a small tourist resort but the nearby Aigues-Mortes still retains a medieval atmosphere within its circle of walls which brings to mind the knights that set sail from here on the Seventh Crusade. As always in Provence, the past is an integral part of the land where nature has created such a variety of landscapes.

86 top Seagulls are among the most common birds in the marshland, while the avocets, with black and white plumage and upturned beaks, are rarer. There are also the unmistakable stilt-plovers with their thin, long legs.

86 center The elegance of the pink flamingos never fails to enchant those who observe these splendid birds, which at times are over three feet and a half tall. Their mating season is particularly fascinating.

86 bottom An egret resting on the back of a Camargue horse. The Camargue is one of the most beautiful nature reserves in Europe, boasting hundreds of species of birds and plants.

86-87 and 87 top left At dawn and sunset the Camargue marshes, including the vast Etang de Vaccarès, take on fantastic colors: pink, yellow, red, purple. The pink flamingos, immobile on their long legs, seem to be enjoying this magic moment.

87 top right Canals and ponds are flanked by spontaneous vegetation that lends a wild character to this land. There are low shrubs such as saltwort and mock privet, as well as plants adapted to salty earth that are sometimes covered by the water in the winter. Around the marshes, the reeds protect the birds' nests and offer shelter to other animals.

88 top
Pink flamingos are the most fascinating sight in the Camargue. These marvelous birds take flight suddenly, their long legs stretched out horizontally and their long, thin *necks pointing upwards. Their ideal habitat are the brackish water marshes, where they lay their eggs and stick their heads underwater in search of plankton and small invertebrates.*

88-89 and 89 bottom right   Most of the lagoons in the Camargue, such as the Etang de Vaccarès, are fantastic natural reserves inhabited by over 300 species of birds, many of which winter here. Teals, for example, are among the ducks that live in the marshes. In the Pont de Gau Ornithological Park at Saintes-Maries-de-la-Mer, which is open to the public, visitors can see most of the species that live in the Camargue.

89 top left and top right The coypu, a rodent much like a small beaver, is a habitué here. Boars and red foxes also live in this zone. The small frog perched on a rush seems to be wary, ready to dash away from any creature that might think he is a tasty morsel.

90 top left
Until not long ago, Saintes-Maries-de-la-Mer was a fishermen's village, but in the last few decades it has become a famous tourist locality. Despite the modern restaurants and hotels, the town has preserved some of its characteristic features.

90-91 Saintes-Maries-de-la-Mer is famous for the huge gypsy festivities held every year on May 24-25. Gypsies come here from all parts of Europe to celebrate their patron saint, Sara. The climax of the ceremonies is the procession, in which the statue of St. Sara, surrounded by the different gypsy clans, is taken on a boat to the beach.

90 top right and 91 top and bottom The solitary homes of the gardians *(cow tenders) crop up here and there amid the natural surroundings. These Camargue "cowboys" never move away from the prairies. On the roofs is a cross, the same one the* gardians *wear around their necks. On holidays the girls wear the traditional red and black costumes of their village.*

91 center The austere Romanesque church in Saintes-Maries-de-la-Mer, built in the 12th century, looks like a small fortress. Some architectural elements were added in later centuries, such as the clocher peigne *and the* tour haute, *a kind of tower that was used as a lookout for enemies and at the same time was a landmark for sailors.*

92-93 Aigues Mortes means "still waters," indicating that the region was once a huge swamp. Massive crenellated walls with towers surround the town, which in the past had a fortified port that Louis IX had built to protect the departure of the Crusaders.

*94 top and 95 top
Built along the
Durance river, the
village of Sisteron has a
medieval center with
winding alleyways and
beautiful old houses
with picturesque
stairways. The village is*
*dominated by the
citadel, which was
entirely rebuilt in the
late 16th century by
order of Henry IV and
contains a fascinating
13th century castle and
the 14th century Notre-
Dame chapel.*

*94 center The
countryside around
Sisteron is brightened
in the summer with
the color of
sunflowers. Besides
the characteristic
small Provençal
houses, the village has
manor houses such as
the Hôtel du Rocher
in the de la Baume
quarter, and the
Domenican church
founded in 1248, a
splendid example of
Cistercian
architecture.*

*94 bottom
The Barcelonnette
valley, which links
Provence and
Piedmont in Italy,
was isolated and
relatively unknown
for a long time. The
town, at 3609 feet
above sea level and
blessed with mild, dry
climate, is
characterized by an
area of luxurious
villas built in the
early 20th century by
the inhabitants who
had become rich after
emigrating to
Mexico.*

L eaving the coast, one travels inland to find the other Provence, the one loved by writers like Jean Giono and Alphonse Daudet who were born here and explored every corner of it on long walks through its mountains, valleys and canyons.

Everywhere, the changing scenery is dominated by olive trees on the sunny slopes of the hills; the Mediterranean maquis, which has replaced the forests on the limestone slopes of the Alpilles and Mont Sainte-Victoire, consists of bushes, berries and flowers from which the bees make the best honey in France.

First, Haut Provence, which begins with the charming village of Moustiers Sainte-Marie famous for its pottery. In the heart of the hamlet criss-crossed by a maze of alleys and small squares, stands the Musée de la Faïence in the Place du Presbytère where an interesting collection of ceramics from the most important workshops through the ages is displayed. Small 17th century townhouses welcome the visitor in the ancient village of Manosque, many times described with graphic poetry in the books of Jean Giono. To the north, Sisteron is an intact medieval village on the banks of the river Durance, dominated by a fort that overlooks the surrounding mountains and valleys. Traveling upstream, the visitor enters the valley of Barcelonnette that connects Piedmont to Provence by way of the Maddalena mountain.

94-95 At the foot of the spectacular de la Baume limestone cliff, the village of Sisteron is divided in two by the Durance river. The historic center lies around the Notre-Dame-des-Pommiers cathedral, built in the 12th century in Provençal Gothic style with Lombard influences.

"Nothing is more romantic than the mixture of these rocks and these chasms, of the green water and these purple shadows, of this sky blue like Homer's sea, and of this wind that speaks with the voice of the dead," wrote Jean Giono about the gorges of Verdon. The rock walls are 2300 feet high and drop sheer into the green water of the river below. A road runs along the top of the ravine with terraces that look down into the abyss while, at the small village of

Rougon, there is a look-out tower that gives a magnificent view over the huge canyon at the point where the river Verdon meets the Baou.

In contrast to the spectacular scenery of this gorge, there are tiny villages all around Provence, perched on rocky hill-tops or nestling in the hollows of valleys filled with cherry blossom, with simple grey stone houses, the inevitable fountain playing in the village square, and shady streets filled with the thousand scents of Provence on market day. Their romantic atmosphere has always made them a perfect setting for love stories, as, for example, for Yves Montand and Simone Signoret who met for the first time in Saint-Paul-de-Vence.

96 At the junction of the Napoleonic and upper Verdon roads, La Castellane, along the Verdon river, is dominated by an incredible rock bluff crowned by the Notre-Dame-du-Roc, which was rebuilt in the 18th century. From here the view of the town is superb.

97 left The Verdon river, whose name derives from its bright green color, is flanked by dizzying rock faces. The most fascinating part of the river, which is 109 miles long, is the gorge known as the Grand Canyon du Verdon, a fissure in the rock that offers a marvelous landscape: cliffs, ravines, grottoes and suspended terraces.

97 right A road along the gorge affords visitors spectacular views and the chance to see boats going down the tranquil river. In the 1970s, 200 paths were marked out on the rock faces for climbers.

Being a meeting point for painters, Saint-Paul naturally attracted the collectors and art dealers whose lives revolved around fashions in art. The most famous of all, Aimé Maeght, created the Collection Maeght in 1964, a museum set amongst olive trees entirely dedicated to 20th century art with internal rooms and a superb open air space where works by Mirò, Kandinsky, Brancusi and others are displayed. The Collection Maeght has made the cobbled village of Saint-Paul, with its small crafts shops, a highly popular tourist attraction. Visitors wishing to enjoy the village's ancient Provençal character that has fascinated so many artists, have to wait until evening when the roads empty of traffic and the silence of the night is only broken by the sound of footsteps and the splash of water in the fountain in the square. Of its historical heritage, Saint-Paul has preserved the defensive walls built by François I in 1536 to protect the village from the attacks of Emperor Charles V.

Another fief of the counts of Provence during the Middle Ages was nearby Biot that sits on top of the hill overlooking the Brague. Its position and simplicity of life made it a great favorite with artist Fernand Léger who moved there from Paris to work on a farm in the middle of the countryside. There he produced paintings, tapestries, pottery and sculptures that today are displayed in the museum that Biot has dedicated to him where the farm used to stand. Local craftsmen who produce pottery and stained glass exported around the world have taken their inspiration from the dazzling blues and white that predominated in Léger's work. As steadfast as Saint-Paul, Grasse, the medieval capital of east Provence, has been the perfume capital since the 17th century. It is said that Maria de' Medici was responsible. Unable to stand the smell of the washed hides at Grasse, she suggested to the tanners that they perfume their products. The suggestion was taken up as the surrounding countryside, being bathed in sunshine and sheltered from the cold, was highly suitable for the cultivation of the jasmine, orange, rose, lemon and lavender plants from which the perfume could be made. Essence of violet has always been produced at Tourrettes-sur-Loup, a village built on top of a limestone promontory, which seems wrapped in a bright violet mantle in spring. The fame of Tourrettes is also linked to the 15th century castle and to the tiny roads from the houses, which act as a bulwark against potential enemies. Sudden views can be glimpsed between one house and the next and the flower-covered balconies look over a gentle slope covered with olive trees. The olive is such an important tree that should it be necessary to uproot one to build a house, the owner is obliged to replant it elsewhere.

99 bottom Grasse, the perfume capital, was the fief of the counts of Provence and is a charming provincial town that boasts a well-preserved historic center featuring buildings with wrought-iron balconies and the lovely Notre-Dame-du-Puy Romanesque cathedral. Place aux Aires is still the home of a picturesque flower market that dates back to the 15th century.

Rivaling Tourrettes as the source of the best olive oil in Provence is the area around Aix-en-Provence. The oldest olive presses are found at the foot of Mount Sainte-Victoire at the gates of Aix.

Arriving in this area, the visitor's thoughts immediately turn to Paul Cézanne who was born here. He had a small house built at Bellevue right in front of the mountain because he liked to paint it at different moments of the day under all the colors and shifts of light. It is the trembling of the leaves of the olive trees that accentuate the particular brilliance of the light in the Alpilles, a series of small mountains with jagged white and grey peaks less than 1640 feet in height. From on high they seem to protect the village of Saint-Rémy, the village that dates back to Roman times and which was painted by Van Gogh many times during his stay there from 1889 to 1890. The meeting point for travelers on this road is Les Antiques at Glanum where one of the oldest triumphal arches from the Gallic and Roman world stands. It was built during the reign of Augustus to celebrate the size of the empire. Standing right beside it in a marvelous state of repair is a mausoleum, said to be of Augustus's grandsons, Caius and Lucius, decorated with splendid bas-reliefs on the four walls and statues of two illustrious persons wearing togas.

Built on the banks of the river Ouvèze, Vaison-la-Romaine also boasts ancient ruins. The addition of "Romaine" to the town's name only occurred in 1924 when wonderful Roman ruins were brought to light by abbot Sautel supported by the Vaison-born industrialist Maurice Burrus, who shared a surname with Sextus Burrus, the prefect of Emperor Nero. The remains were of a similar quality to the House of the Dolphin at La Villasse where large quantities of oyster shells and fish-ponds attest to the prosperity of those times. Then there is the large and beautiful House of the Messii in the district of Puymin where the elegant vestibule leads into the atrium built with a typical central *impluvium*. The Roman theater was built against the hill with the stage cut out of the rock; it is a little smaller than the theater in Orange which is the venue for the international summer performances of song and dance known as *Choralies*. Another of Vaison's Roman attractions is the House of the Silver Bust which boasts mosaics and marbles and takes its name from the statue found there but now kept in the local museum, the Musée Théo-Desplans. Medieval Vaison, the upper city above the river reached by crossing the Roman bridge, was built during the 13th and 14th centuries using stone from the Roman remains. The narrow, twisting streets were almost deserted at the start of the 20th century but began to fill once again when the excavations began to unearth the architectural treasures that have attracted tourists from around the world.

102 top In the heart of the valley, Lourmarin is dominated by the Renaissance castle. Here we see its exterior and the fireplace salon. The complex comprises the old castle, built in the late 15th century, and the new castle, which dates back to the mid-1500s.

102 bottom Les Baux is divided into two areas on a rocky plateau. On the top is the citadel with the ruins of the castle belonging to the Baux, the most powerful liege lords in France until the 15th century; below it is the village proper, rich in Renaissance buildings and small museums, which is a great tourist attraction.

Like the Alpilles hills, the landscape of the Val d'Enfer is colored white and grey but it is harsher and its limestone rock seems to bristle with innumerable pinnacles. This is the valley onto which the fantastic village of Les Baux faces, apparently planted on a rocky plateau surrounded by wild vegetation. The spectacular ruin of the citadel looms over the valley which, during the Middle Ages, used to belong to the lords of Baux, the most powerful vassals in the Midi who claimed to be descended from King Baldassar, one of the three wise men. The village built during the 16th century with the intention of giving Les Baux its ancient splendor stands below the castle in the heart of the citadel. Today the village is invaded by tourists every summer. In order to appreciate its character and the architectural details of the Renaissance buildings, you really have to arrive early in the morning or at sunset. Wan-

dering through streets like Rue des Fours or Rue Trençat, one comes across the Hôtel des Porcelets that is now the home of the modern art museum, the Hôtel de Manville with an exhibition of ancient engravings and prints. More nostalgic and charming is nearby Fontvieille, a tranquil provincial village with a traditional square reserved for games of *pétanque*. Close by stands the famous windmill that inspired Alphonse Daudet in *Lettres de mon Moulin* written in Paris in 1869. Although he had moved to the capital after a family financial disaster, Daudet always hankered after his homeland and returned there in his heart, as did his boastful hero, Tartarin, to the nearby Tarascon in the book Aventures Prodigieuses de Tartarin de Tarascon read by children around the world. Tartarin's village is ringed by walls with a long central road flanked by a portico. The town also has one of France's loveliest fortified castles with interior in flamboyant Gothic style that was built at the end of the 15th century by King René.

If Tarascon is now a small city, the Lubéron in the heart of upper Provence is a zone where many small typical Provençal villages still exist, with a square protected by plane trees where the locals meet up over a glass of *pastis* and where the flower, fruit and bric-a-brac markets are held. Often, an old manor-house will stand over the village as a reminder of its feudal past, for example, in the enchanting village of Lourmarin with the *chateau vieux*, built between 1495-1525 and the *chateau neuf*, designed after 1540.

103 left The Fontvieille mill, which inspired Alphonse Daudet's Lettres de mon Moulin, *continues to arouse curiosity. In reality this work was written in Paris, where the author's family had moved.*

103 top right Perched on the sides of hill in the heart of the Lubéron mountains is Bonnieux, a rich papal city until the French Revolution whose ascending streets and 16th, 17th and 18th century buildings bear witness to its former splendor.

103 bottom right Saignon, the stronghold that once controlled access to the Pays d'Apt, is one of the most characteristic villages on the northern side of the Lubéron mountain range.

One of Provence's most beautiful roads leads from Lourmarin to Apt where the ochre color of the land signifies Roussillon clay which is extracted pretty much everywhere. This section of Provence is like Colorado for the color of the earth, which changes from yellow, to pink, to orange, to red and to a vivid violet, and for its jagged and contorted limestone towers crowned by a piece of rock like the head on a mushroom that suddenly appear as one turns a bend in the path.

A few miles on lies the village of Ménerbes that became famous after publication of the book *A Year in Provence* by the English author Peter Mayle which was translated into seventeen languages. Ménerbes has been the scene of many important historical events: as a refuge for Protestants, the citadel was besieged innumerable times and has witnessed many massacres. A road through the open countryside takes the visitor to Oppède-le-Vieux, one of the Lubéron's most characteristic villages, which overlooks orchards and fields of sunflowers. After a long period of abandon, it was returned to life during the 1970s thanks to the efforts of Parisians who built holiday homes out of the ruins. Equally lovely is Bonnieux, shaped like a pyramid surrounded by pine trees that stretches up towards the sky at the foot of the Lubéron regional park.

104 top, 104-105 and 105 top right Gorges, cliffs, galleries and panoramic terraces with an overwhelming view: in Roussillon, in the Pays d'Apt, the color of the land ranges from yellow to pink, orange, red, and bright purple. This is the reason why the ravine between Rustrel and Gignac is called the "Provençal Colorado."

105 top left and bottom right Ochre is extracted everywhere around Roussillon. Once it was used to paint walls with, but now it is utilized in the cosmetics industry. Visitors can hike along marked paths in search of the "fairies' hats," incredible conical limestone formations that suddenly crop up amid the vegetation.

106-107 and 107 right Clinging to a hill among olive and almond trees, the village of Gordes, with its light-colored stone houses, was "discovered" in the mid-1900s by the Hungarian painter Victor Vasarély.

Towering over the village is the 12th century castle with battlements that was rebuilt during the Renaissance. In the hall of honor there is a magnificent stone fireplace decorated with sculpted acanthus leaves.

Dominated by reddish stone and brick, Gordes seems to appear suddenly from nowhere, surrounded by dozens of small orchards separated from one another by dry-stone walls built with the precision of a watchmaker. The ancient construction technique is demonstrated at neighboring Les Bories, an open-air museum of mysterious huts built in dry-stone at some unknown time. A superb panorama over Vaucluse is visible from the center of Gordes.

107 top left Les Bories, situated in the middle of the countryside southwest of Gordes, can be reached via a path flanked by many low stone walls. The

origin of the dry-masonry houses in this village may even date back to the period when the Ligurians abandoned Vaucluse many centuries before Christ.

107 bottom left The two sackcloth puppets in this photograph seem to be humorously announcing the arrival of Provençal spring.

108 top left and center
The yellow of the sunflowers which Van Gogh loved to paint explodes in mid-summer, while the fields among olive and apricot trees are laced with the fiery red of the poppies.

108 bottom left
The geometrically patterned fields at the foot of Mount Ventoux are both enchanting and peaceful.

108 right For those who love to hike, there are marked paths among the lovely meadows and woods that lead to Mount Ventoux, on the summit of which are meteorological stations and telecommunication apparatus.

109 Near the Sénanques abbey, the village of Gordes, perched on a hill, has revived its former splendor since it was discovered by intellectuals and

artists such as the painter Vasarély. The light-colored and well-restored stone bastides, or country houses, are the dominant architectural feature in this area.

Protecting the valley brightened by the colors of the vegetation – the vivid violet-blue of the lavender, the yellow of the sunflowers, the red of the fields of poppies and the variegated expanses of wild flowers – stands majestic Mont Ventoux with its peak crowned with white stones. Petrarch climbed to the top of this mountain in 1336 with his brother and two servants but wrote laconically, "A mass of rocky, wild and almost inaccessible land."

The green spread that lies at the feet of Mont Ventoux takes its name from the village of Les Barroux, a labyrinth of medieval lanes that faces alone onto the plain of Carpentras.

The best view of the neatly kept vineyards is from the large round towers of the village castle built by the local lords in the 12th century; it stands alone and majestic, proud of its dominant position.

110 top left A beautiful garden surrounds the Petrarch Museum at Fontaine-de-Vaucluse. It is located in a house built in 1927, on the site where the great poet stayed many times during his sojourn here from 1327 to 1353.

110 top right Ancient Roman ruins are to be found everywhere in Provence. This Roman fountain is an evocation of the canal the Romans built to channel the water of the Sorgue river to Arles.

110-111 The old water wheel on the Sorgue river at Fontaine-de-Vaucluse harks back to the time when its wooden blades raised the water from the river to produce hydraulic energy.

111 top left Known as "the little Venice" because of the many canals of the Sorgue that cross it, Isle-sur-la-Sorgue has in the last thirty years become the second most important town in France for antiques after Paris. The unused areas, called "villages of antiques," host the antique exhibitions featuring hundreds of dealers.

Although Mont Ventoux disappointed the poet, the nearby Fontaine de Vaucluse with its "clear, fresh waters" inspired him to write the most famous of his poems dedicated to Laura, the woman he had met in a church in Avignon on April 6, 1327. The clear spring is the source of the Sorgue, the river that flows around the small town of Isle-sur-la-Sorgue, a true paradise for antique lovers. It all began thirty years ago when Albert Gassier, a *pied-noir* from Algeria, established the first flea market in this enchanting area of France known as the Venice comtadine for the many canals that cross it. Today there are more than two hundred antique shops and dealers that open their shops on the weekends selling paintings, rustic kitchen cupboards, fabrics and garden furniture among other things. On Easter Day and August Bank holiday, the village becomes a tangled mass when stall-holders arrive from all over France to present their antiques along the large Avenue des Quatre Otages. By crossing a small bridge, one can enter Bouigas, the oldest district of the village, with its tiny streets that still go by their ancient names: Rue de l'Orme, Rue de l'Ecrevisse and Rue de l'Anguille. They are all names of fish because the village used to be a center for fishermen after the count of Toulouse gave permission in 1327, confirmed by Pope Julius II in 1508, for the waters of the Sorgue to be fished. The practice, unfortunately, died out at the end of the 19th century when an epidemic killed nearly all the fish.

111 top right Isle-sur-la-Sorgue, in the middle of the Sorgue river, which is divided into two branches at the partage des eaux (partition of the waters), is one of the most typical towns in Provence. The river was once so rich in fauna that its shrimp, eels and umbrine were served at the popes' banquets in Avignon.

111 bottom right Paintings, old chairs, lacquered chests of drawers only a few decades old, chinaware, glasses and old picture frames: the antique dealers have just about anything you want here. The "village of antiques" is open on weekends and Monday, and on Sunday the junk dealers also have a great deal of objects on display on the quay.

112 left and 112 bottom right The Pays de Sault is part of the so-called violet triangle on the Albion plateau

between Sault, Séderon and Banon. In this enchanting valley the period between May and August is a blaze of

colors from flowers that is unrivaled in the rest of France. In the land of lavender, besides the marvelous and

inevitable blue and violet, one can easily see expanses of red poppies and multicolored meadows of alfalfa.

Mont Ventoux is at the center of the *Triangle Mauve* on the plateau of Albion between Sault, Séderon and Banon, which is covered by a carpet of lavender between June and August in a gorgeous blend of shades of blue and violet.

The local inhabitants are so proud of their production that represents 70 percent of the French lavender market; about fifteen years ago they created a fraternity to protect lavender cultivated to a certain quality. The members of the order wear a mauve cloak and cocked hat. August is spent in a series of festivals dedicated to the valuable violet flower. Sault offers a popular two-day festival that includes parades of carriages, sales of products and a lavender scything competition.

The most spectacular view of lavender is seen by the visitor to the abbey of Sénanque, the Cistercian abbey founded by St. Bernard in the 12th century. Its walls were built from pink stone and the roof is still covered with the original grey flat stones. It stands out against the sky and an unending expanse of perfumed violet. The simplicity and strictness preached by Bernard seem to have found some compensation in the grace of the flower as it gently sways in the wind.

112 top right and 113 Southeast of Mount Ventoux is the Pays de Sault. In July, everything is carpeted with lavender and permeated by its lovely scent. The dry plateau and sandstone-limestone earth are ideal for

cultivating this splendid flower. The village of Sault, 2510 feet above sea level, affords a fantastic view of the valley as far as Mount Ventoux. On August 15 there is the annual lavender festival.

114 *You will discover old, fascinating villages at the foot of Mount Ventoux. Among these, in the middle of the cultivated hills, is Le Barroux, a tiny village at the foot of a Renaissance castle* *built by the Baux, the local liege lords. It was rebuilt in the late 16th century and restored in the early 20th century. It is now the home of the Center d'Etudes Historiques et Archéologiques du Comtat.*

115/118 *One mile from Gordes, in a narrow valley, the Cistercian abbey of Sénanque stands out among the lavender fields. This is the most beautiful of the three abbeys in this area, the other two being Sylvacane and Thoronet.*

119 *Around Le Barroux the vineyards alternate with the olive and apricot groves. From the castle in the background there is a* *view of the Carpentras plain and the Alpilles Mountains. A few miles away is another enchanting village at the foot of Mount Ventoux— Malaucène.*

120-121 *The Sault valley is almost circular. Here the green of the olive and almond trees stands out among the blue-violet lavender. The* *best lavender is grown at an altitude of 2000-4600 feet and is distinguished by its leaves and color, which tends to be more violet.*

122 top left The stars of the local fairs are the santons, *the small statues used in the traditional manger scene, handmade by craftsmen who hand down their art from generation to generation.*

122 center left and bottom Christmas is the most solemn holiday for the Provençal. Before going to midnight mass, the family has the gros souper, *Christmas Eve dinner.*

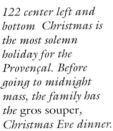

122 top right For Christmas the locals create a tableau vivant *of the manger scene, a very moving event that takes months of preparation.*

123 The santons, *the* crèche *statuettes, are made of terracotta and are painted and dressed in traditional regional costumes. Representing the most characteristic figures and trades, they evoke life in the old Provençal villages.*

A s a land of legends and folklore, Provence loves to relive its past in magnificent festivals celebrated in costume with traditional dances to the sound of traditional music. Frédéric Mistral, the poet from Arles who was awarded the Nobel prize for literature in 1904, was a great supporter of the Provençal language and helped to create the Arlaten Museum in the city of Arles which offers an admirable cross-section of the region's traditions. The museum displays examples of traditional dress and clothing that are still described by Mistral's own handwritten captions. There are models of the holy manger where Jesus was born with the characters made from glass; this tradition originated when a Venetian noblewoman married a duke of Nevers during the 15th century and brought the art of glass-spinning to the area. Then there are the living amulets that, it was believed, protected one from illnesses, like the snail, the slime of which was supposed to prevent measles. The most interesting room is undoubtedly the one that reproduces the atmosphere of the large Christmas *souper*, the meal eaten on Christmas Eve, which is still celebrated in many families. The table is laden with thirteen desserts, one for each guest at the Last Supper, including almond nougat, hazelnuts, dried figs, grapes, dates and oranges. The rest of the menu comprises baccalà (dried salted cod) cooked with herbs, and different dishes of local vegetables like cauliflower and thistle seasoned with olive oil taken from the first pressing or a white sauce based on anchovies.

Christmas is preceded in Provence by the large *Foire aux Santons*, which is held in Marseilles, along the Canebière, in Arles, in the cloisters of Saint-Trophime, at Les Baux and at Fontvieille, the homeland of Tartarin de Tarascon. The *Santons* (the handmade terracotta statues used in representations of the Holy Manger) are painted and dressed in local costume by *santonniers*, the craftsmen whose art is handed down from father to son. At Aubagne, the center of the santonnier tradition, there is a huge variety of figures: the shepherd offering a lamb, the housewife with a large black hen from which broth is made that, it is said, is excellent for the new-born, and characters that represent figures from the past: the baker selling flat bread, the garlic seller, the fishwife and the fisherman carrying his nets. Around these central figures stands a miniature Provençal village with a well, dovecote, oven and mill. The story goes that these Christmas representations in the houses of Provence date back to the times of the French Revolution when, following the ban on Midnight Mass, the Marseillais decided to celebrate the birth of Jesus in their own homes using terracotta figures. Midnight Mass is still celebrated in some villages as it used to be in ancient times, for example, in the collegiate church of Saint-Martin at Saint-Rémy, where the ceremony of the *pastrage* is renewed each year with the presentation of a lamb by shepherds from nearby villages and the priest tells the story that commemorates the long trip made by the shepherds two thousand years ago to render homage to the Lamb.

The land of Tartarin, Provence relives the dark moments of the Saracen raids with triumph and a lively martial spirit when the procession in honor of the patron saint was accompanied by a military escort of the so-called *Bravades*. That era is commemorated each year at Saint-Tropez on the Sunday before Ascension Day when inhabitants of all ages form a division of troops that recalls those companies of soldiers of fortune. Preceded by music, the modern day soldiers march through the city streets escorting the statue of Saint-Tropez and firing off rifles and pistols. Every self-respecting *Bravade* ends the day singing, drinking and dancing traditional dances.

124 The bravade *is an evocation of the battle-scarred past of Saint-Tropez, which over the centuries defended the gulf against invaders. The celebration on May 16-18, which is particularly dear to* the locals, coincides with the patron saint's feast day. In the past the word bravade *indicated the military escort used during the religious procession to protect it from Saracen raids.*

125 left The participants in the bravade *parade take out their old, brightly colored traditional costumes handed down from father to son, which are fit out by the* Oustau de la Bravade *seamstresses. In June, the second* bravade, *the Festival of the Spanish, commemorates the victory of Saint-Tropez against the Spanish galleys in 1631.*

125 right The bravade *begins with the consignment of the flag to the captain and his senior officers. Then sailors and musketeers accompany the bust of Saint-Tropez in procession through the town, which is decked with red and white flags, while there are cannon-shots and salvoes, which are interrupted by the authorities' salute and the tribute to the French Navy ships.*

127 top left and center At Arles, bullfights are a tradition that is a passion with the locals, as they are in Seville or Ronda. The Easter and September Feria events, which are held in the Roman amphitheater, feature famous matadors such as Victor Mendes. In the past Luis Dominguin was the most highly acclaimed toreador, and Pablo Picasso was a regular spectator, in search of inspiration for his paintings. The Feria also includes the novillade, a kind of baptism of fire for young matadors.

In spring, the Camargue celebrates the Ferrade, the day on which one-year-old bulls are branded in a festival that mixes work and fun. The event is of great importance as these are the bulls that will be used in the bullring at Arles at Easter and on the first Sunday of July when the matadors attempt to show their skill in running the bulls through. But there are also bloodless corridas in which the toreadors are required to remove a *coccard* from the lyre-shaped horns of the bull.

126-127 and 126 top Branding bulls when they are one year old is a fundamental moment in the life of the manade, the Camargue ranch. The gardians (cowboys), on horses specially trained to lead herds, grab the wild bulls by the horns, isolate them from the herd, throw them to the ground and brand them with hot irons. This event becomes a festivity in which the entire ranch takes part. Sometimes the ranchers allow tourists to participate in the branding (ferrade), which ends with a huge dinner.

127 bottom left and right At Easter, beside the traditional Spanish bullfight, there are the courses camarguaises, bloodless but exciting spectacles in which ten razoteurs dressed in white must tear off the red cockades that are wrapped around the horns of six bulls.

128-129 and 128 top left In honor of their black patron saint, St. Sara, on May 24 and 25 gypsies come from all over Europe to Saintes-Maries-de-la-Mer. The festivities commemorate the arrival on this beach, aboard a boat without oars or sails, of a group of persons exiled from Jerusalem, including the Virgin Mary's sister and the mother of the apostles John and James. According to tradition, St. Sara, queen of the gypsies, was there to welcome them.

During May, Arles also celebrates its *gardians*, Provençal cowboys and *guardians* of the herds. The horseback *gardians* are dressed in leather trousers and check shirts and hold a trident in one hand as they parade through the town to the admiration of women dressed in the traditional costume depicted in the paintings of Van Gogh.

The gypsy festival celebrated at Saintes-Marie-de-la-Mer on May 24-25 in honor of St. Sarah is famous around the world. Patron saint of the gypsies, Sarah took in the three Mary's chased out of Judaea. On the eve of the festival, the reliquary of the saint is carried in procession to singing and acclamation. On the following day in a riot of colors and sounds, gypsies from all over Europe carry the statue of the saint right down to the sea to symbolize the welcome offered by Sarah to the three women who miraculously reached the town via the Mediterranean. On the next day, an immense procession of *gitans*, *gardians* and citizens of Arles in traditional costume take the saint's boat to the seashore to be blessed.

128 top right and 129 top left On the eve of the commemoration, amid songs and applause, the reliquary with the remains of St. Sara is taken out of the chapel with the aid of a hoist and ropes. The following day the statue, accompanied by the gardians *and women dressed in costumes, is borne in procession to the seashore to commemorate the welcome reserved for the fugitives from the Holy Land. The next day St. Sara is immersed in the sea and is then taken back to the church.*

129 top right The gardians *take part in the procession on horseback and dressed in traditional costumes, acclaimed by the crowd. These cowboys, who tend their herds with a trident in hand, are the protagonists in Arles of a festival in their honor that takes place in early May.*

129 top right, center right and bottom During the Saintes-Maries-de-la-Mer festivities there are also many events in the amphitheater, in which the horsemen of Camargue proudly display their skill.

130 top Tartarin and his prodigious adventures is the main character in Alphonse Daudet's best-known work, Tartarin de Tarascon. The author, who hailed from Nîmes, spent almost all his life in Paris, but the recollections of his youth were always an important part of his writings.

130-131 The Tarasque, one of the oldest festivities in Provence, takes place in late June. It harks back to the legendary time when the inhabitants of Tarascon were terrorized by a winged monster that looked like a huge turtle, which came out of the Rhône river every year and tore children to pieces.

Music, songs and a tremendous social atmosphere are also to be found during the bottle procession on June 1st at Boulbon. The main characters are the men that head for the church with a bottle of wine in hand to have it blessed in the chapel of St. Marcelin; the women, meanwhile, prepare a feast at home enlivened by hallowed wine.

One of the oldest festivals is the Tarasque, codified by King René in the 15th century during the last weekend of June at Tarascona. It recalls the time that knights battled heroically to destroy the winged monster of the Rhône that came out of the river each year to tear young men and women to pieces until tamed by Saint Martha. Today, the papier-mâché Tarasque leaves its lair and winds its way along the city streets, to the amazement of children and the entertainment of their parents, whipping its tail from side to side and making the girls scream.

On the night of St. John's day, many villages celebrate the Nuit de la Saint-Jean, which has marked the summer solstice since the distant past. As darkness falls, the night is lit up by fires of all sizes as a hymn of joy that the summer has arrived.

INDEX

Note: c=caption,
bold type=main entry